All Skate
True Stories from Middle Life

by Lori Jakiela

Roadside Press

Contents

The Art of The Take-Off..1

The Art of The Carry On 2

You Can Tell a Lot About People from The Way They Behave on Airplanes.....14

Le Petite Butt 19

Portrait of a Bathing Beauty at 72 36

Of the Wolf 44

Kurt Cobain Knew Nothing About Love......................................51

There Never Were Snakes in Ireland..56

Pick Yourself Up Off the Ground 60

Love Saves the Day..66

A Christmas Season in Flour 70

Soft 74

Portrait of a Young Artist in Suburbia 78

In Here, Life is Beautiful..83

Boy Crazy, or Sex and Death from Kindergarten to Grade Eight 88

Enlightenment in Blue 93

Kindness is Its Own Memory 101

Wonder. Sunbeam. Bread. Loaf. 107

Family History Of X 119

What a Doll.. 125

Hopeful Things.. 128

Spring Cleaning 137

P.S.. 142

Publication Notes 146

About the Author 147

"I realize there's something incredibly honest about trees in
winter, how they're experts at letting things go."
—Jeffrey McDaniel

"I've never felt so powerful and so calm. I just don't care,
because I'm too old. It's such a great feeling."
—Emma Thompson

"The fact was I didn't want to look my age, but I didn't want to
act the age I wanted to look either. I also wanted to grow old
enough to understand that sentence."
—Erma Bombeck

"I still have the roller skates from *Boogie Nights*."
—actress Heather Graham, a.k.a. Roller Girl

For Newman
Let's go around again. Again. Again.

The Art of The Take-Off

My favorite thing about flying is take-off. I love the rev of the engines, the feel of throttling down a runway at 600 miles an hour. The miracle of that. I love the way the landing gear lifts and locks into place—slam dunk, no turning back. I love the magic-carpet whoosh of air beneath my feet. I was a flight attendant for years, trained to pay attention to every sound and motion—the whir of wing flaps, the thrum of the hydraulics, the way ascent feels, the steep smooth climb, the gravity-defying beauty of that. I loved and still love every impossible thing about flight. I love the way something so heavy can become, in an instant, seemingly weightless. If something so huge can go airborne with the weight of all those human hearts wrapped up inside, anything is possible.

The Art of The Carry On

A grown man took a swing at me in the Tampa airport. It was 5 a.m. I know it was 5 a.m. because I remember sneaking coffee, against my airline's regulations, which I'd hidden behind the ticketing podium.

It's hard to forget a grown man taking a swing, especially when it comes before noon.

I was a flight attendant, taking tickets and saying the usual, "Hi, welcome aboard," when this man approached with his suitcase. He didn't look like the kind of guy who'd take a swing. He was dressed in a tan business suit. He was only moderately tan. Sure, he used a lot of hair gel, but this was Tampa, not West Palm, and there's a difference.

***

An aside:

Flights between my base, New York City, and West Palm are called Miracle Flights. When it's time for boarding, wheelchairs line up like taxis at an airport cab stand. People who need extra time for boarding—parents with small children, famous actors who don't want a fuss, people in wheelchairs—get to board first.

We call these passengers pre-boards.

Pre-board, boarding before you board, doesn't make any more sense than any other airline catch words and phrases—*rough air* for turbulence, *trip* for hijacking, and of course, *deplane*.

If deplane means to disembark, then plane would mean boarding, right? Let's all plane now.

Ready, set, plane!

"De plane! De plane!" Herve Villechaize, the diminutive actor who preferred to be called a midget and who played Tattoo on the classic 1980's TV show *Fantasy Island,* would shout at the beginning of every episode.

"De plane! De plane!" Herve Villechaize shouted in commercials for Dunkin' Donuts after he was fired in 1983 during *Fantasy Island's* final season.

Herve Villechaize was fired for demanding equal pay with his co-star Ricardo Montalban and for harassing and propositioning women on set. The sign on Herve Villechaize's dressing room door read, "Sex Instructor–First Lesson Free."

Back then, pre-Me Too, reporters called the sign cheeky. They called it almost cute.

***

When I was first hired by my airline, the company store sold t-shirts that read: "Marry Me. Fly Free." The t-shirts were a hot item, always sold out, such were the sensibilities of America in the 1990s.

Later, I'd use the t-shirt slogan on my soon-to-be husband, though he wouldn't bite. His idea of dream travel–Pittsburgh to Ocean City, Maryland. Ocean City, Maryland to Pittsburgh. There are no flights between Pittsburgh and Ocean City, Maryland. It's a seven-hour drive, more or less, depending on stops at Wawa. Wawa has a great meatball sub. Wawa has clean bathrooms. The coffee, as convenience-store coffee goes, isn't terrible. My would-be husband loved Wawa, but he hated to fly. He still does. He isn't much for travel. We got married anyway.

And I'll be happy here and happy / there full / of tea and tears.

That's the poet Frank O'Hara, beloved on this earth. Two decades in, my husband and I are still married, and we both still read Frank O'Hara, who loved to travel, who loved the ocean, who also said:

I am really a woodcarver / and my words are love.

***

But back to pre-boards, a word Frank O'Hara would love I think, a word that maybe should be translated to pre-planes in airline semantics.

Pre-boards get the best overhead bin space. Pre-boards get first dibs on flight attendant call buttons, which they press again and again, hoping for a pre-flight water or juice or a nice Bloody Mary, extra spicy.

I have to take a pill, doll. I'm dying here, doll. (Makes choking sounds, hands around throat.) Be a doll, doll. Slip me a little something extra, know what I'm saying?

Later comes the miracle:

By the time those flights land in West Palm, nearly all the pre-boards' ailments are—praise be!—healed. The passengers who just a few hours ago couldn't walk a jetway deplane like gymnasts, their pockets and carry-ons stuffed with vodka minis and sleeves of Biscoff cookies they snatched from the beverage cart, while a fleet of wheelchairs—pre-ordered by the pre-boards—stand by, empty, waiting.

***

As for the New York-Tampa flights, those are usually okay.

***

When people say Florida Man, they should have to say which Florida, which who, which where, which why and which how. It's all in the details, but these recent headlines keep going general on Florida while mixing in the specifics of the crime:

- Florida Man Attacked by Squirrel During Selfie with Squirrel
- Florida Man in "No, Seriously, I Have Drugs" T-Shirt Arrested for Possession of Drugs
- Florida Man Suspected of Using Private Plane to Draw Giant Radar Penis
- Florida Man with Handlebar Mustache Assaults Woman on Plane, Starts Fight With Several Passengers, Yells at Police to Tase Him "And You'll See What Happens," Gets Tased 10 Times

As for my Tampa Florida Man, he seemed mostly normal, other than the suitcase he wanted to bring onboard. The suitcase was huge and heavy, with glittery ribbons tied to the handle to make it easy to find in the stew of humanity that is baggage claim.

The ribbons meant my Florida Man had flown enough to know the power of glittery ribbons. The ribbons meant he feared losing his suitcase. The ribbons meant he could find what was his before it vanished.

***

Once years ago, I took a bus from Pittsburgh to Vermont. Somehow, during my switch from one bus to another, my suitcase was lost. I spent half a week in Vermont at a pinky-up writer's conference in my bus-appropriate, non-pinky-up MTV Rocks sweatpants, Ramones t-shirt, and borrowed socks.

It seemed weird that Greyhound could lose a suitcase, a bus being a simple mode of ground transportation, different from flying, definitely less complicated, a matter of class, privilege, or just gravity maybe.

"Now everyone can fly the flying bus," senior flight attendants, who previously worked for luxurious but defunct airlines like Pan Am and reminisced about the years when flying was an exclusive, glamorous, white-gloves-and-caviar affair, said.

They flapped their hands like wings and sighed their pigeon sighs.

When I was flying, senior flight attendants worked First class or Business class. Coach class, mostly called Coach, no class attached, was for newbies like me.

"To the back with you," senior flight attendants would say, as if working in coach was a punishment or a rite of passage, both. They'd flap their hand-wings then, too.

***

In Vermont, at that writer's conference, I felt ashamed. I didn't have money to fly, so I took a bus, 17-plus hours. I'd been accepted to the conference on a scholarship that was, in part, based on the fact that I had no money. I looked a mess, partly because of that luggage problem and my lack of fancy pinky-up clothes, but it was more than that. Like what had happened to my luggage was a metaphor. Like I, a working-class kid from rust-belt Pittsburgh, had landed, an alien, in the country of Ben & Jerry, Robert Frost, tennis whites, prize-winning cows, and literature with a capital "L."

Losing my luggage meant losing things that might have allowed me to blend in: my carefully curated writer clothes (black turtlenecks, black jeans, black everything), red lipstick, scuffed Doc Martens, some hair gel even—not Florida level, but still.

Without my luggage, I felt vulnerable, exposed.

A fraud.

***

"A writer's job is to get naked, to hide nothing, to look away from nothing, to not blink, to not be embarrassed or ashamed," the great grit-lit Florida writer Harry Crews said.

But Harry Crews was a regular on "The Tonight Show." Harry Crews wrote what some people, including me, say is the greatest memoir of the 20th century—*Childhood: Biography of a Place*. Harry Crews cut his hair into a mohawk. He had many tattoos. One tattoo said, "How do you like your blue-eyed boy Mr. Death?"

Harry Crews, in a series of interviews called *Getting Naked with Harry Crews*, said, "So you get a tattoo like this and a 'do like this, and wear a shirt where the tattoo shows, and you walk into a room of people and feel the animosity, the disapproval, the how-dare-you. You can feel it coming off them like heat off a stove. And the thing I want to ask them is, how have I deserved this, what have I done that so offends you?"

***

"Sir," I said to the Tampa man with the huge suitcase, "I can check that for you. That way, you can relax and you won't have to worry about finding space on board."

The man looked at me as if I'd offered to gate-check his only child. He looked at me as if I'd told the worst-ever Florida Man joke.

"I'm happy to help," I said and gave him my best Welcome Aboard smile. This probably made things between us worse.

***

The airline I worked for had, still has, an infamous acronym: Don't Expect Your Luggage to Arrive. The acronym's tricky, like all acronyms maybe, but easy to figure out if you try, and funny only if it doesn't apply to you and your bags.

This acronym is especially not helpful when dealing with passengers determined to board with their luggage and whatever's inside.

***

The Tampa man's suitcase may have been filled with pork bellies. It could have held a prize-winning pig. This was around Christmas. You'd be surprised how many people pack hams in their carry-ons around Christmastime and treat said hams like kilos of cocaine, something illicit and essential and valuable beyond reason.

Or his bag could have been filled with more suits that he'd need to impress the people he was headed to meet.

Maybe he needed the suits for a funeral.

Or maybe, like another man on another flight, his bag held something more precious and unpredictable than any of that.

That man came into the galley. He pointed to an apple I'd brought for lunch. He said, "I thought there wasn't any food on this flight."

I said, "I brought that from home."

He said, "Huh. Really," and kept staring at the apple.

Ravenous, or just spiteful, angry, entitled, who knows. People pay a lot of money to fly. They pay a lot of money to be denied a snack or a drink or even a terrible meal featuring a stale breadstick and a chicken breast with fake grill marks.

Something, they might as well say, *just give us something to make this all feel worth it.*

About the apple, I said, reluctant, my voice all as-if and you've-got-to-be-kidding-me, "Well, you can have it. If you want."

I thought he'd pass on the apple, because really, who eats another person's apple? I had a 12-hour day ahead, no time for real food, and so the apple mattered in a way it wouldn't have otherwise. But the man didn't pass. He grabbed the apple and bit. And bit. And bit.

He seemed so hungry, like he'd been lost on a deserted island and our plane picked him up and this apple was the first real food he'd seen in who knows. Apple juice ran down his chin. He swiped it with his shirt sleeve. I handed him a bev nap, proper placement even, the airline logo facing out, such is the training of a flight attendant.

Everything my airline taught—proper bev nap placement, the pronunciation of cheeses in first-class, how to handle a hijacking or worse—was essential to my job. Everything my airline taught was delivered with the same level of intensity. Would you like a beverage? Would you like ice? How about some oxygen? Can I offer you a little CPR?

"Everything matters when you think nothing matters," my in-flight instructor said, a catchphrase. I'm still not sure what she meant, but she said it with such heart it seemed, still seems, important, a life lesson maybe.

"Would you like some pretzels?" I asked the man who gnawed my apple to a brown nub. "We have a stash up front."

The man nodded. He said he didn't have time to eat before. He said he hadn't been eating much lately and now, who knows why, he was starving.

"I hate flying," he said, "but my mother wanted me to bring her home."

He blotted the apple juice off his chin. His eyes teared up. I handed him another bev nap. Then another.

You never really know what's happened to a person. You never know what's in someone else's heart, the baggage they carry. In this man's case—his mother's ashes.

In this man's case—grief that outweighed his fear of flying.

***

"Sir," I said to the Tampa man with the oversized bag filled with what-not, "I'll just need to check and weigh your bag and make sure it will fit on board."

And that's when he swung.

He didn't say anything. He just tried to roundhouse me.

I ducked, its own kind of miracle, one of the few things my in-flight instructor never taught me. My morning reflexes are pretty much sloth-in-a-tar-pit, but maybe, through some airline-train-ing-infused intuition, I felt the punch coming.

***

My Tampa man was ranting when airport security took him away. He called me the kinds of names that are hard to hear, es-pecially at 5 a.m., especially from a stranger, especially when the words echo down a lush tropical concourse and everyone turns to stare.

Maybe terrible things happened to him earlier. Maybe he stood in a long line at ticketing. Maybe he was frisked by the TSA. Maybe he paid $6 for a stale airport cookie. Maybe he was carry-ing the ashes of someone he loved. Maybe he was headed some-where he didn't belong and was nervous about it.

"Don't get too big for your britches," my mother used to say when she thought I was aspiring to be uppity and overstepping my roots.

She wanted to protect me, I think. Maybe. Maybe not. "Stay in your lane." My mother said that, too.

But this is about the Florida man who took a swing at me.

I know only one thing for sure: this man did not want to be separated from his bag.

Whatever was in there was so important to him that he'd risk anything.

***

Attachment to material possessions, the Buddhists say, is an obstacle to enlightenment. Attachment to material possessions, the Buddhists say, is a detour from one's authentic self. Attachment to material possessions, the Buddhists say, detours one's spiritual journey.

Maybe at that pinky-up conference all those years ago, I was forced by fate or Greyhound to be my authentic self, no costume to hide behind. I was in my 20s, though, vulnerable as a bruise, trying to become whatever I'd become. I would have loved to punch whoever lost my luggage and left me exposed like that, with nothing more than the words I'd write, none of which were very good.

Oh, boo hoo, Harry Crews would say.

"Strip it down!" Harry Crews said, "Let's get down to where the blood is, the bone is. Instead of hiding it with clothes and all kinds of other stuff, luxury!"

I believe that. I hold onto beautiful madman Harry's words beyond reason. I have no idea what the man in Tampa all those years ago believed or needed or wanted to hold onto beyond reason. I'm older now and try to be gentle, more understanding. I fail daily.

Some Tuesdays, I go to the basement of a library in Oakmont, Pennsylvania, where three lovely Tibetan monks in saffron robes lead a community meditation. We meditate on the difference between loving kindness and love. One is selfless, one is not.
During our meditations, we wish everyone healthy.
We wish everyone peaceful.
We wish everyone, including ourselves, well.

***

Still.
Who takes a swing at someone at 5 a.m.?

I wonder if Tampa guy remembers and feels bad about things. I wonder how big his fine was or if he was put on a no-fly list or if he got off with a warning about how it's wrong to punch a flight attendant, especially before noon, especially before said flight attendant had enough coffee to fuel a punch back.

This was the 1990s, after all.

The world was less scary and more forgiving then.

***

Still.
Tampa guy?
Fuck that guy.

You Can Tell a Lot About People from The Way They Behave on Airplanes

Jimmy Carter boarded the plane with the other passengers. This was 1999, the end times according to Prince, Jehovah's Witnesses, and other end-times prognosticators. I was a flight attendant who wanted to be a writer. I was a writer who wanted to spend her life as a flight attendant—rootless, only loosely connected to a world that might be ending soon.

Jimmy Carter stored his small bag in the overhead, then made his way through the cabin. He stopped at every row to shake hands. He shook hands with crying children and beaming grandparents. He shook hands with expensive-suited business-humans, who for once looked up from the work they carried like boulders and seemed almost moved.

He shook hands with the pilots, gate agents, and other flight attendants. He shook hands with me.

You can tell a lot about people from the way they behave on airplanes. The ones who hit their call lights and demand lobster and martinis, the ones who follow the safety demo like they're studying for a chemistry exam, the ones who put their seatbacks all the way back, the ones who tattle on the ones who put their seatbacks all the way back, the ones who kick and knee the seatbacks that are just a little bit back, the ones who go on rants that show up on YouTube, the ones who record said ranters being duct-taped and handcuffed as they try to bite their fellow passengers and flight crew, and so on.

"Airplanes are human test tubes," a flight attendant friend said. "And humans are failing the test."

I was a flight attendant for seven years, from 1994 until 2001.

On this day, in the 1999 end-times, Jimmy Carter, the former president of the United States, that sweetheart, was on a flight I was working. It was a shuttle flight, D.C. to New York, I think. No First Class, no fuss.

Jimmy Carter's handshake was sturdy but sweet. His hands were familiar—not the soft hands of privilege I expected from a leader of the free world and not the hands of my father or the other Pittsburgh working-class men I knew growing up, but not distant either.

"Honest hands," my grandmother called hands that carried a callous or two, hands that have done some work and therefore carried their own maps of what it means to be human and vulnerable in this world.

I was a child when Jimmy Carter was president. What I remember most is that my father, who voted for Richard Nixon, voted for him. My mother, who didn't vote, said that if she did vote, she'd have voted for Jimmy Carter because he seemed nice and his wife was fashionable and pretty.

"I like her hair," my mother, who loved Jackie Kennedy and her sweet suits, said about Rosalynn's up-do.

People who didn't vote for Jimmy Carter called him "the peanut farmer." I didn't understand why that would be a bad thing. His brother Billy was funny and brewed beer. His wife Rosalyn had some problems, but she and Jimmy loved each other in ways my parents never did. It was 1979. There was a gas crisis. There was a hostage crisis. There was an energy crisis. Jimmy Carter put on a sweater when he asked America to put on sweaters and turn their thermostats down. Jimmy Carter, arguably the most powerful man in the world, was so gentle that, when attacked while jogging by a rabbit, the prey of this world, he didn't fight back.

The Washington Post made jokes about it.

What Jimmy Carter wanted most was peace when it seemed everything around him was burning. What Jimmy Carter offered was honesty in a world built on lies.

"Good men make shitty presidents," my father, who believed the world was corrupt, said.

The older I get, the more I believe that, too.

The older I get, the more I refuse to believe that.

"Hope is the thing with feathers / that perches in the soul," Emily Dickinson said.

"This election is a battle for the soul of America," CNN talking-head Wolf Blitzer says now in 2024, our most recent end times.

Back in the 1900s, Ronald Reagan beat Jimmy Carter.

Prince survived 1999, but he died in 2016, an overdose of painkillers. He died alone in an elevator. People made, still make, jokes about it. They quote lyrics from his hit "Let's Go Crazy"—*when the elevator tries to take you down.*

Dearly beloved.

Back in the 1900s, Ronald Reagan beat Jimmy Carter.

It's worth repeating, maybe.

Ronald Reagan told a lot of jokes during his presidency. Here's one:

"It's true that hard work never hurt anyone, but why take a chance?"

Jimmy and Rosalynn Carter first led a group of Habitat for Humanity volunteers in 1984. They built 19 homes in New York for families in need of safe, affordable housing in what became known as the Carter Work Project. Jimmy and Rosalynn Carter continued building and advocating for affordable housing alongside Habitat for Humanity for almost four decades.

"You can tell a lot about a fellow's character by his way of eating jellybeans," Ronald Reagan, a jellybean afficionado, said.

You can tell a lot about people from the way they behave on this earth, and around animals, and on airplanes.

Rabbits, by the way, are fierce when threatened. I know. I have a rescue rabbit. Her name is Waxy Kardashian Newman. Waxy, to honor her birth name, which honors her birthplace, Waxahachie, Texas. Kardashian because Waxy Kardashian Newman is a big rabbit, but she's mostly all butt. *I like big butts and I cannot lie,* Sir Mix-A-Lot sang. This is the song I sing to Waxy Kardashian Newman when I bring her a rabbity treat shaped like a hamburger or ice cream cone, or some organic lettuce, or a chunk of high-grade hay.

Waxy Kardashian Newman is spoiled and, as all rabbits are, adorable. Still.

You should see her teeth and nails.

Back on my flight, Jimmy Carter said, "Hey there," and "Good to see you," like everyone was a friend. He asked, "How are you?" and waited for an answer. He looked everyone in the eye and held us in his gaze like we all mattered. He wasn't going to stop until he'd greeted everyone on that plane.

When it was time for pushback, when we couldn't wait anymore, the captain came on the PA and said, "We need everyone seated. Even you, Mr. President."

Jimmy Carter blushed and waved. He apologized—to the people he didn't get to, to the captain, to the other flight attendants and me, to his secret service agent who probably ate Tums for breakfast, such would be the worry of guarding a man so bent on being open to everyone and everything in this life.

Jimmy—never James—Carter, the great former president of the United States, a saint on this earth, said he was sorry to hold us up.

He said he didn't want to be any trouble.

He said, "Well, I guess we'll be going now."

Le Petite Butt

"I wasn't really naked. I simply didn't have clothes on."
—Josephine Baker

"What is this butt?" my friend Constance wants to know, but she says "boot."

Constance is from France. Her real name is Ursula. Ursula goes by Constance when she's in the States. It's easier on Americans, Constance says, who thinks anyone named Ursula must be a Disney villain.

We're in a T.J. Maxx dressing room, where the T.J. Maxx slogan, "Get the max for the minimum," plays between indecipherable elevator music that probably has been test-marketed to make American consumers like me buy things. Knock-off perfumes. Designer socks. Plastic lawn flamingoes, Himalayan salt lamps, lavender-scented candles—all designed to make wherever you land seem like home.

Constance has never been in a T.J. Maxx.

She looks around at all the detritus Americans pass off as French that is not French—French press-on nails, cosmetic cases covered with cartoon French bulldogs, French coffee presses stacked next to mugs emblazoned with French poodles, clothing from a brand called French Connection.

"French Connection," Constance says with disdain, "is British."

"The British," Constance says, "know nothing about fashion." She's right. See the Royals and their hats that could double as bird feeders. "Mon Dieu," Constance says and sniffs.

But this is the United States, and Constance and I are here in this discount store with bad lighting in a dressing room that smells oddly like corn chips, to try on bathing suits.

All around us, other women are doing the same thing.

"How does my butt look?" one says.

"Does my butt look big?" another one says.

"Is my butt hanging out of this?" one says, and another says, "Oh dear God."

Constance is modeling a bathing suit the size of a sandwich baggie. Her butt is tiny and adorable as a macaron. She twists and squints, tries to examine herself from behind as the fluorescent lights buzz and snap overhead.

Constance says, "What is this fuss?"

She says, "A butt is a butt."

She says, quieter, "Americans," and sounds like she's flicking mosquitoes, but gentle-ish in her own lovely French way.

Then she looks at me as if to say sorry, as if to make me, with my own big American butt, exempt.

***

I am here to find a suit that will not make me look like a beached manatee, though I love manatees, those floating potatoes, those gentle smoosh-faced sweethearts.

I am here to find a suit that will allow me to walk from beach towel to water without feeling embarrassed of everything my adult body has become and keeps becoming.

"Le cul borde de nouilles," Constance says and sniffs again.

"It's an expression," she says, and smacks my butt, but gentle-like.

Translation: *Your rear end is surrounded by noodles.*

It's a compliment, I think, maybe. With Constance, it's hard to tell.

"You're lucky," Constance says, but I don't see it that way.

Cellulite, stretch marks. Self-tanner might help a little, but ultimately, no.

"No," Constance says, "*lucky* lucky. As in life. As in we are here together, now. That luck."

Constance smacks my butt again, harder this time.

***

I do not, on most days, feel lucky.

I have never won more than $5 in the Pennsylvania lottery. I know lucky people—my friend Carol, who won her entire wedding and honeymoon in Jamaica; my cousin John, who, after playing the lottery for decades, finally hit a million, though he had to split it four or five ways, but still. John is legendary in my family, evidence that all Jakielas can be winners if we just commit to the bit.

I've won two things in my lifetime: a Ouija board at a Catholic church bingo, which my mother, a devout Catholic, made me burn because Ouija boards invite the devil in, and a boxset of poetry CDs, which I think my mother would have found as questionable as the Ouija Board if she had known.

The poetry CDs included the first-ever recording of Walt Whitman's voice. "I am large / I contain multitudes." But that wouldn't have impressed my mother and later that same recording was used in a Levi's jeans ad, which I don't think Walt Whitman would have liked much.

"So it goes," my beloved Kurt Vonnegut, who was maybe lucky because he survived the bombing of Dresden and lived to write about it, might say, but still.

***

Constance and I are flight attendants. This month, we've been working the same line, New York to Vegas, the red eye. She's older. I'm not. I love her age, how gorgeous she is. I chalk it up to Constance being French, but it's probably just genetics. Still, I aspire.

All the times I've been in Las Vegas, I've come home with a stale airport Cinnabon, low self-esteem, and not much else.

On our last layover, Constance won $50 from a slot machine called "Haywire." She used the $50 to buy us both champagne at the hotel pool bar, where I refused to take off the black dress I used as a cover-up, even though it was, in Vegas terms, about 140-plus-whatever degrees Fahrenheit.

Constance splashed around in the pool. She swam underwater, graceful as a seal, and heckled me from the deep end.

"What is it you say?" she said. "Oh! Chicken!" She made chicken "bawk bawk" noises that sounded somehow elegant and French.

If you've traveled, you know. Dogs, chickens, every animal sounds different when translated into the language of their home.

In German, dogs say "wuff wuff." In Italian, dogs say "bau bau." In Polish, "hau hau." In Russian, "guv guv." And in Constance's native French, it's "waouh, waouh."
Wow.
Wow.

***

Today, I especially do not feel lucky here in 20th-century America, in a T.J. Maxx dressing room, under bug-zapping fluorescent lights, in a mirror that reflects what I've started to think of as my own mortality.

Everything that was here is now there, gravity, gravity.

"I was so beautiful once," my mother would say, astonished at pictures in old albums, her own self, lovely on a beach in a green two-piece, looking sexier than any 1950s pin-up.

My mother would hold the pictures up to the light, examining, as if they were pictures of strangers, people she didn't recognize. Deep fakes.

"I wish I'd known," my mother said, as if she were talking about a lovely friend she wished she'd been kinder to way back when.

"Be kind, babies," Kurt Vonnegut advised, and I always thought he meant be kind to others, but maybe kindness starts with the self.

Most days, I lean, as they say, into the darker angels of my nature. That's Abe Lincoln, though, and not Kurt Vonnegut or Whitman, though Whitman loved Abe Lincoln most of all.

"I sometimes buy a bikini," Susan Lucci, that iconic star of American daytime TV's *All My Children*, said. "But I'm too shy to wear one."

Susan Lucci's mother was one-third French, which according to Constance, doesn't count.

"Pfft," Constance says, and waves a hand like she's swatting flies.

***

Susan Lucci, supermodel gorgeous, was nominated for an Emmy 19 times before she finally won. Her character, Erica Kane, a beloved villain Lucci played, slapped other characters 28 times, stabbed or clubbed other characters at least nine times, and once dunked a character named Annie Chandler's head in a toilet, an act followed by Annie Chandler stabbing Erica Kane.

For 41 years, the lovely Susan Lucci played a woman who was, in every way, fearless.

"My weakness is my shyness," the real Susan Lucci, who never wore a bikini in public, said.

"Waouh waouh," the French dogs would say.

***

This might seem superficial, all this talk about bikinis and bodies, but let's go deeper.

My mother said about her own shy beach pictures: "Why didn't I ever know I looked like that? I didn't look so bad."

My mother said, "I looked pretty good back then."

My mother said, "I was probably okay."

My sweet, tough, funny mother, who never knew her own beauty. My mother, whose sisters would make her hide in the attic when their boyfriends would visit because they were terrified their boyfriends would fall in love with my mother because she was that beautiful.

My mother said, "I was so backwards," a Western Pennsylvania expression that means, in part, shyness and, in a bigger part, regret.

"Puritaines," Constance says of American shyness, mine, Susan Lucci's, my mother's, and rolls her lovely eyes.

Not so long from now, I'll look at pictures of myself from a few or more years back. I'm wearing a white bikini, a hot pink bikini. I won't recognize myself. I have never been photogenic, but even in pictures I hated and hid at the time, now I think I looked, in my own mother's words, okay.

"Sweet Mary Joseph and Jesus, just take the picture," my friend Sinead always says. Sinead is Irish, with that wonderful sensibility that comes from her tribe. "You'll never be younger than you are right now."

Glamaireacht is the Gaelic word for barking.

It sounds glamorous.

***

I want to tell Constance this is about something bigger, mortality, about understanding how short our lives are while we're still living them. But it's also about vanity. To deny that would be a lie. But to be alive, maybe, as a mortal on this earth is, in itself, vain.

"I see you beauty and you are mine," Hemingway wrote about a lovely young woman he saw in a cafe in Paris.

Hemingway wrote the woman into a book. He froze her, in that moment, so she would stay that way forever, even after he looked up from his notebook, even after she had vanished.

Later, people would accuse Hemingway of lookism, sexism, but I think what he did was an act of love, not just for the young woman, but for all of us.

Who doesn't want to go on forever, beautiful, amen?

Glamaireacht. Even if it means barking, it sounds lovely.

"I see you beauty," Hemingway wrote.

And everyone who reads his *Moveable Feast*, that love letter to his first beloved wife Hadley and to Paris, sees that beauty too.

***

Look, right now. Take the picture.
See how lovely you are?
You'll never be as young as you are in this moment.
Take the picture.
Again.
Again.

***

"Americans," Constance says, in that breathy-cigarette way of hers, which means Americans think too much or too little or that we don't understand anything at all.

I think Constance is here, in this dressing room in a discount store in an American strip mall, because she's doing observational research, the way Hemingway in that cafe did observational research.

She wants to capture, the way Hemingway captured, the fleeting loveliness of what it means to be alive, maybe. I love my friend, but Constance is not Hemingway, not so romantic, and Constance isn't Sinead, with her lovely Irish humor and cynicism.

I think what Constance really wants is to understand:

a)   American women's obsessions with body image

b)   The trauma of bathing suit season in these United States

c)   American women's tendency toward self-loathing in all its forms

d)   The cultural significance of this

Significance, signified, signifier—all those French ideas American literature professors push on poor graduate students.

Dear Simone DeBeauvoir. Dear Sartre.
Deconstruct this.
Help us all.

***

My first week in grad school, where I'd gone to study poetry, I spent days crying in my tiny apartment. I filled my bedroom with used Kleenex and crushed cans of Diet Coke and empty cartons of Ben & Jerry's Chunky Monkey, which I ate by the pint with a spoon.

I didn't understand the words the other graduate students were using, all of them culled from French literary theory, all of them as foreign to me as T.J. Maxx dressing rooms seem to Constance.

Constance studied Latin at the Sorbonne. "American literature professors," Constance says, "are stupid imperialists."

"Americans," Constance says, "can never understand existentialism."

"Americans," Constance says, "understand ice cream."

"Ben and Jerry!" I say. "Vermont!"

"Yet you don't know to savor, *la savieur*," Constance says, the French word sounding so much like *savior*.

Then Constance acts out American gluttony, an invisible spoon shoveled again and again into her rosebud mouth.

La savieur.

A friend, who once aspired to write advertising copy, wrote this for Ben and Jerry: "Life is short. Eat the pint."

"Mon dieu," Constance says.

Savor. *Savieur.* Savior.

And so it goes.

***

There's something called The French Paradox Theory. The French, despite their love of things like rich cream sauces and brie cheese and butter and wine, have low death rates when it comes to coronary heart disease.

"La savieur," Constance says, is the secret.

Savor this life.

Every bit.

***

 "I am never eating again," a woman in the dressing room next door says. "Not now. Not ever."

I tell Constance about American fad diets–Keto, cabbage soup, green cleanses. "For your research," I say, joking but not.

America runs on diet pills and artificial sweeteners. I tell Constance my favorite bit of American dietary trivia.

Sylvester Graham, a Presbyterian minister and Puritan, one of the *Pruitaines* my friend instinctively loathes, invented graham crackers in part to ward off masturbation and other sins.

A Graham cracker. Just a touch of sweetness, not too much. Just enough to sustain a life, but not too much pleasure, could ward off danger. *God crackers*, people called grahams.

Grahamites, Sylvester's followers, believed in temperance, cold baths, hard mattresses, and vegetarianism. Graham's movement flourished in the 1830s, right up until he died in 1851 of complications from opium enemas.

"What is so scary about sex that you eat crackers that taste like shit?" Constance wants to know.

Constance squints her lovely face. "And what is this enema?" she says.

I tell her I'll explain it later and pick the bathing suit I'm trying on out of my butt crack.

***

Sylvester Graham was 57 years old when he died from, some might argue, complications of self-denial and loathing.

Constance and I are in our 30s.

More than half-way there in Graham years.

Constance sighs in French, all smoke and world-weariness.

***

Once when I was in Paris, I went to a club called Aux Trois Mailletz. The Three Mallets. Inside the club, a staircase led down into a cave. In my memory, the cave was packed. I wove through the crowd to a seat at a long table. I had no idea what I was doing. I tried to make myself invisible, visible, both.

A woman so beautiful she glistens in my mind still, was dancing on the table, part belly dance, part burlesque. She was singing a song I didn't recognize in the French I did not and still do not know.

When she bent down and touched my cheek, when her lovely hair brushed my shoulders, I shivered. I remember shivering, not from lust but from being overwhelmed by her beauty, her fearlessness up against my own fear.

She probably did this show many times every week. I hope she was paid well, but considering that this was Paris, in a country that values work and the people who do it, I think she was.

The walls of the cave were the walls of a cave. Remember Plato, his allegory, how easy it was to become mesmerized by a tiny flickering light and forget the outside world, the sun?

The woman on the table in front of me was so lovely, dressed in tiny silvery scarves that reminded me of moth wings.

Moths, so drawn to light they'll die for it. A woman so lovely she was both moth and light.

Later, I'd go into other caves. I'd go to the famous catacombs of Paris, where the skulls and bones of the dead are stacked like produce.

In the catacombs, there are skulls stacked in the shape of hearts. There are bones stacked to make archways like rainbows. There are bones stacked to spell out words I can't decipher, except "Mon Dieu." That one's easy. Poor God. My God. So many of us calling for mercy in so many languages, so many of us calling out for help or just to be seen.

"Do not remove any bones or be cursed forever," our guide said before we descended. He laughed a laugh that was more of a fly buzz, an insect wing, then he went serious. It was hard to know if he was joking about the curse or not.

I did not remove any bones, though I put my finger into the bullet holes in more than one sad skull. I have no idea why. Maybe it's the same reason I always want to touch dinosaur bones in Pittsburgh's Carnegie Natural History Museum, where I've been scolded by docents for doing exactly that. Maybe it's the reason I sometimes stop at the gravesite of Arco Politano, born 1876, died 1886, and touch his tiny headstone in the Catholic cemetery in Irwin, Pa.

I think this all has something to do with the experience I'm having with Constance, in T.J. Maxx, in the year of our Lord 1998, the 1900s, but I'm still sorting that.

***

"Oh dear god, no," the woman in the dressing room next door says, as if she's translating.

A Latinate root is a Latinate root.
Mon dieu
I've heard a lot of French phrases in life, from my friend Constance, in songs by Edith Piaf, in cartoons, specifically Pepe Le Pew, the lovesick Looney Tunes skunk who took the concept of "love stinks" literally and often invoked God in his scent-imental pursuit of his beloved Penelope.

See what I did there?

"Scent-imental," I say to Constance. "Dad joke."

But I can't explain to my French friend why I'm telling a Dad joke when I'm not a Dad. Or what a Dad joke means, not really. Or why I'm thinking about Pepe Le Pew in this dressing room without offending my French friend with French stereotypes perpetrated by a cartoon skunk.

In those Looney Tunes cartoons, Penelope was not a skunk. Penelope was a black cat with an accidental white stripe painted down her back.

Penelope, the cat, hated Pepe's desperation, his insistence, but more than that she hated the smell of skunk, which was, maybe, a gesture toward Americans who think Europeans, with their armpit hair and distrust of deodorant, seem a little off.

Constance smells spicy and does not shave. Her breath is a little rancid, even though her teeth are perfect pearls.

Constance says, "You have hair like my mother," and she holds some strands, twists them around one of her red-tipped fingers, the moons of her nails left clear like tiny test tubes half-filled with blood, a true French manicure.

I think she's going to say something nice, but she says, "My mother used a cigarette to burn the ends."

Constance is beautiful as a paint stroke. She's brutal as a virus, but what I love about her is the honesty. The limits of language make it difficult for her to lie in English. I don't know about her French.

The times I've been in France, I apologized a lot. My manners were, I think, good because I can't say much more than *merci* and *pardon* and *champagne*.

I, like many Americans, am mostly monolingual. I am embarrassed of this, yet I don't do the work to improve myself. Lazy, of course, but mostly I'm embarrassed. It's terrifying to speak like a child, to grope around in the dark for words I need. It's arrogance, of course. I speak American English with some passable street Spanish and a spattering of phrases that can help me find bathrooms and beer around the world.

All of this makes me feel worldly when I am, mostly, the village idiot in many countries other than my own. I rely, as Blanche Dubois in *A Streetcar Named Desire* did, on the kindness of strangers.

In France, people were beyond kind. They treated me as if I were a child, innocent and clueless.

Once I wore denim overalls to dinner at the Eiffel Tower and the maître d' out of pity gave my friend and me a window table. Later I got my foot stuck in a Metro door, despite the signs featuring a cartoon rabbit with a big throbbing foot that was supposed to illustrate that the doors, in fact, did not bounce back. Another subway rider helped pry me loose. Then he patted my head like I was a poodle that was not French.

*****

Traveling in Paris for the first time in my adult life, I was not responsible for my own failures. I liked this very much. I pointed to coffee—signified, signifier—and someone would hand me coffee.

I pointed to menus and food appeared.

If I wanted to navigate a grocery store, I followed someone who looked like they knew what they were doing.

I bought the same cheese, the same wine, imitating every movement as if I were one of the mimes I saw in Luxembourg Gardens and which I presume are both French and existential and universally creepy, though Constance might say otherwise.

The cheese I bought could have been the French equivalent of Velveeta. The wine could have been Mad Dog. It didn't matter. I was happy. At the checkout, the cashier helped me sort my cash.

Nearly everyone seemed kind.

Forget everything you've ever heard about French arrogance. There is no single sweeping way to understand humans.

If I could speak better French, or if I wasn't so afraid to try, I'm sure I'd come across as more myself, and I'd be much more difficult to tolerate.

I have no idea how Constance's personality translates back home in France.

When are people most themselves, with the power of language or without it?

***

Once, years later, when Constance was sad, she sent me a note.

She wrote in English, "I am all sorrow. I need a big arm to wipe this tear," as if her whole body were a tear, all that water under the skin, a water balloon, a vessel for every stashed sadness.

I wrote back in English to say I was sorry, that I understood how she felt.

I wanted to pick good words that could close the distance between us, but I went with standbys.

"We all feel sad sometimes," I wrote. "Things will get better."

My handwriting was fat and open, as easy as the words that tumbled out. A light in a cave leading nowhere. Constance is much braver than I am. She's not afraid to work to find the words to say what she means.

"If the butt is so consuming," she says, "eat lettuce."

Portrait of a Bathing Beauty at 72

Just a few months before she died, my mother did something she hadn't done in years. She put on a bathing suit. The bathing suit was a flowery one-piece with a tiny flounced skirt and a built-in push-up bra for beach cleavage. My mother was 72 years old. For decades she'd sworn off beaches and bathing suits.

"Who in their right mind would want to look at this," she said, and jiggled everything that jiggled.

"Imagine," she said. "A bathing suit. At my age."

But then our neighbors, three sweet kids who had doubled as the grandchildren I had so far denied my mother, asked her to join them in their backyard pool. That summer had been hot. Our neighbors had been persistent. My mother loved them very much.

"Come on, Bertie," they said. "Just a little dip."

My mother also loved fun. Even in her 70s, she bought herself toys. Her latest purchases—a Tickle-Me Elmo and a dancing hip-hop duck she bought at the dollar store that played "I like big ducks and I cannot lie"—made her giddy.

"What will they think up next?" she said. She poked Elmo's tummy. She wound up the duck and let it rip.

"Isn't that a hoot?" she said.

My sweet sad mother, so hungry for simple joy.

She turned our neighbors down until she couldn't turn them down anymore. Then my mother drove her little red sports car to JCPenney, rooted through the sale rack, and came back with something she could manage.

"It's sensible," she said about the suit, a solid one-piece covered with flowers. "Nothing that leaves my ass hanging out."

My mother was a double-D, so the suit's push-up bra was important.

"With a little boost, these make a good tray table," my mother said, and pretended to balance a glass of iced tea on her boobs.

About getting comfortable in her new suit, my mother said, "Well Rome wasn't burned in a day."

My mother, mixologist of metaphors, who'd spike a cliche into the ground like a football and call it a hole-in-one.

My mother by all accounts had a blast that day in her very sensible suit, although there are no pictures to prove this.

"She told us she'd kill us if anyone came near her with a camera," one of our neighbors said.

The suit was still hanging on a clothesline in the basement after my mother died. My husband talked about it when he got up to speak at my mother's funeral. I couldn't speak, grief like a stopper in my throat.

On the memory board at my mother's funeral, there were pictures she picked out. One of these is my mother in a bikini. She's wearing a glamorous sun hat and dark glasses. Her double-D boobs, her dancer's legs, are perfect, no filter, no photo editing, just my beautiful mother on a beach somewhere, looking like a Hollywood starlet.

"There is an age when you are most yourself," the poet Linda Pastan wrote.

My mother was, I think, most herself in that picture. She was most herself with our neighbors, splashing around in their rickety above-ground pool.

"Imagine," people said, would go on saying.

***

I imagine.

***

I imagine being like my mother when I'm 72. I imagine being like her right now.

"That'll show them," my mother said about her bikini picture.

She meant the priests. She meant her prim sisters and neighbors and anyone else who might be offended by flesh and mortal beauty in the presence of death.

But she also meant, I think, to say she was here and beautiful and alive and isn't that fleeting shadow lovely even so.

"I see you beauty and you are mine," Ernest Hemingway wrote.

"There is an age when you are most yourself," Linda Pastan wrote.

Freeze frame.

Freeze.

Cryotherapy, maybe. A way to hold still but go on and on.

Consider Walt Disney's head, stashed in a freezer somewhere, all those rumors and hope.

None of them true.

***

At the mall earlier this week, the Beach Boys played on repeat. Macy's smelled like coconut sweat. Everywhere I looked, preying-mantis skinny mannequins were lounging between racks of hot pink bikinis and dayglo orange tankinis, metallic mono-kinis and suits with names like Miracle and Magic and Control.

I think about that word, control, and what it means to lose it. How freeing it is to lose it.

A Miracle. Magic, even.

Every year, my kids like to go to water parks. This year was no different. The other day, I caught my son Googling Kalahari, America's largest indoor water park and our family's favorite.

"We're riding the Zip Coaster together again this year, right Mom?" he said.

I love my kids more than I worry over my own dignity. I'm nearing 50, and like my mother, I love fun. The Zip Coaster—half rollercoaster, half waterslide—is awesome. Nothing says family bonding like throwing ourselves off a man-made waterfall in a raft that looks like something out of *Land of the Lost*.

Still, the idea of a bathing suit makes me recoil like a Sleestack.

If you're not a *Land of the Lost* fan, Sleestacks are particularly creepy lizard people who hiss in the presence of light, magic crystals, or, simply, grace.

Grace.

We could all use a little, a pass maybe.

***

This bathing suit season, I've gained a few pounds. Motherhood, menopause, mid-life everything.

"Who in their right mind would want to look at this?" my mother said.

In *Land of the Lost*, there's no mother, no wife. I've been thinking about this, how in nearly every Disney movie or made-for-TV after-school special, the mother is dead or missing. Maybe it's because a dead or missing mother raises the stakes. Or maybe it's because a dead or missing mother solves the problem of having to look at an aging woman's body, the effect that would have on ratings.

I try not to think about everything on me that jiggles. I try not to Google anti-cellulite cream.

I Google anti-cellulite cream. It's expensive and mostly caffeine based, and I drink so much coffee daily, I think that should have helped some by now.

I make plans to hit the gym as soon as I can find my membership card, which is probably lost somewhere in my sock drawer, my own land of the lost.

Jergens makes a nice self-tanner. Jergens has been around since 1901.

"We're not here to stop at skin deep," the Jergens' ads say. "We're here to help you feel truly, deeply, skin-to-soul comfortable, with a few surprises along the way. We bottle all that up into the Feel-Good Feeling of Jergens."

Jergens promises a fruity scent that will make Monday feel like Friday, but I'm not sure what that might smell like.

The cartoon character "Cathy" says tanned fat looks like muscle.

***

I've always been curvy, back before Sir Mix-a-Lot and my mother's animated duck liked big butts. I've dreaded bathing-suit season ever since I was 17 and my high school boyfriend convinced me I'd look great in a bikini.

Maybe because my top curves never matched my bottom ones, I've never been comfortable in bathing suits period, let alone bikinis, but I went with him to the store, where he picked out a bathing suit he thought was perfect.

This act is, of course, its own kind of love.

When I got the suit home, I tried it on, not looking in the mirror. I walked out to model it for my boyfriend, who was waiting, excited as paparazzi, to see me in this new and miraculous light.

I tried to suck everything in. It is impossible to suck hips in, not to mention thighs, but flexing helps.

Jergens self-tanner would have been a nice touch, but I didn't know that then.

"So, what do you think?" I said, spinning like a jewelry-box ballerina.

He paused for a minute, then said, "It looks weird. Like someone inflated your butt."

Now here I am, five decades in, my own body a cocoon I should be ready to shed.

I'm not.

I get a bathing suit I think will be passable. I do not look at myself in a mirror.

It still feels scary and humiliating to be exposed like that.

But the good thing about kiddie waterparks is that they're filled with other parents, many of them curvy like me, many of them marked with the cuts and bruises and sags that come with raising and loving small children, the fun and exhaustion and fullness of life that come with that.

"We're easy to spot," my husband says. "It's us and the crack whores. And I think the parents look worse than the crack whores."

The crack whores, he says, are winning.

***

Years ago, when I asked my mother why she gave in about the bathing suit, she said, "Well, they asked me."

She said, "I didn't want to miss out."

She said, "I figured it was time to get over myself."

Yes, I think now. It is.

Of the Wolf

One year, when I was a broke and itinerant flight attendant, I lived in a house with six Irish accountants. The house was in Forest Hills, Queens, a few subway stops from Manhattan.

Having six housemates meant we could almost afford the rent. Having housemates who were accountants meant that everything from the cost of toilet paper to the heating bill was divided up.

My housemates called the heating bill the "oil delivery fee." They used words like gorgeous and brilliant when describing a plate of overcooked spaghetti. They believed, really believed, Guinness is good for you. These housemates—five men and one woman—were Irish citizens. They found work and housing through an underground network that specialized in exporting Irish accountants.

Before this, I'd thought Ireland's chief exports were beer, The Pogues, blood sausage, and jokes about priests and donkeys. My housemates liked jokes, but hated blood sausage. They had many Irish friends in the city, all of them accountants, all of them living with other Irish accountants, all of them able to do long division and recite Yeats while drunk.

A confession: I've always thought of myself as Irish, and so I was happy to pay $600 a month to sleep on a futon on the floor and be among my people.

I'd been adopted by Italian/Polish American parents when I was a year old, and I learned a little about my ancestry, which they sometimes babbled at me. I clung to the Irish side of my lost past. My birth name was Phelan and I wore green on St. Patty's day. I wore a Claddagh ring. I was proud of my Irish eyes and the way they curled into commas when I laughed. I read Yeats and Joyce and knew all the words to "Danny Boy."

Being Irish made me feel special, particularly during my teenage years. My non-Irish parents didn't understand me. How could they? And now, all these years later, in Queens, New York with authentic Irish folk, I thought I would learn who I really was.

"My birth name's Phelan," I told my housemate Sinead.

Sinead was lovely, blue-green eyes, dark hair, a laugh that could crack plates. We became good friends right away, which meant we told each other the truth.

"You're not really Irish, you know," Sinead said and patted my hand like my hand was a puppy. "Americans put on green t-shirts and tennis shoes and say they're Irish and it's just not true. Irish people are Irish. Americans are American."

"She's right," Brian, one of our other housemates, said.

Brian overheard us from the kitchen, where he'd been frying ground meat. My housemates had dinner together at 7 p.m. every night. They took turns cooking. I never saw any of them make anything other than Spaghetti Bolognese. The recipe didn't vary, no matter the chef—three jars of Prego, two pounds of ground meat, two pounds of spaghetti, one loaf of Wonder bread.

When I wasn't flying and it was my turn to cook, I'd try to mix things up. Chicken Romano, tacos, fajitas. But mostly, when I cooked, my housemates would nibble politely, and the next night we'd be back to Spaghetti Bolognese.

"Americans always want to show off and be something they're not," Brian said. He poked his head out of the kitchen and pointed a wooden spoon our way. "That's how you get shamrock knickers. You get *Kiss Me I'm Irish*. You get, Jesus lord help us, green beer. It's desecration. It's not right. To be Irish is to be Irish, and that's the end of it."

Brian was from Dublin. Sinead was from Galway. All but one of the housemates was from the south of Ireland, which meant they shared the same politics and generalized about Americans the way I generalized about the Irish.

One night, after Sinead had downed a few pints and had a fight with Paul the bartender at Yer Man's pub in our neighborhood in Queens, I was driving her home. I don't know why, but Sinead decided to flip off a group of kids on Metropolitan Avenue. She rolled down her window, yelled, "Ho there," and stuck her middle finger out. The kids yelled back. One of them turned around, dropped his pants, and mooned us.

Sinead was, in her own words, gobsmacked.

"A finger," she said, "does not equal an ass. A finger equals a finger. I will never understand you people. Never."

I did not want to be "you people," but there was so much I didn't understand back.

Take our housemate, Tony, for instance.

Tony was from Belfast. This was a problem, since the housemates carried the troubles from their homeland with them. Sinead's fight with Paul the bartender was over something political I didn't grasp. Whatever it was made Sinead, a usually soft-spoken woman, shout.

Sinead's grandfather, I knew, had been a driver for Michael Collins, the founder of the I.R.A. Sinead's family was deeply Catholic. I had no idea where Paul the bartender was from, exactly, or what his religious beliefs were. It would never have occurred to me to ask. Paul had an Irish accent. He worked at an Irish pub. Drunk women took off their bras and donated them to the collection that dangled like tongues over Paul's head. Paul often gave me wooden nickels to use for free drinks. He was kind and funny and called me "Love."

Back at the house, I'd seen the fury Sinead had directed at Paul. It bubbled up whenever Tony was in the room. Tony was built like an eraser, stubby, with a square head and buzz-cut hair. His room was in the basement, next to the washer and dryer. The basement was concrete. Tony's bed was a worn-down couch. Tony didn't talk much. At dinner, he sat at the end of the table, head down. He ate fast, and usually got stuck with the dishes.

One day, because I wanted to understand, I asked a question. I'm not sure exactly how I phrased it, but I wanted to know the state of things between Ireland's north and south. I knew the little I'd learned from history books and Brad Pitt movies, but I wanted to know the more personal side of things. How it affected people. My housemates, for instance.

What happened next was broken. Tony lowered his head even more. The other housemates said some things. Brian said, "Isn't that right, Tony? Isn't it?"

Tony didn't say anything.

Until he did.

I don't remember what he said because it seemed like nothing, really. Maybe he agreed with Brian. Maybe he said he was finished. What was happening at that table was beyond me, though I'd set it off.

Sinead said "That's enough," and Tony went trudging off to the basement.

I wouldn't see him for days.

I had a late flight that night, a Vegas red eye. When I came home, Tony's face was bruised. One eye was leaky and swollen shut.

When I asked what happened, he said, "I don't know what you mean." Then he stumbled back down to the basement.

Later Sinead would say the boys had a fight. They'd been drinking. They'd locked Tony in the basement. There was no bathroom down there, so after several hours, Tony used the washer.

Later, when they unlocked the door and found what Tony had done, they beat him.

"That's the beginning and end of it," Sinead said. "Let it be."

It had been my fault, of course. I felt terrible. I'd like to say something here about privilege, and ignorance, what it does to people, but what it comes down to is my privilege, my ignorance, what it did to Tony and what it didn't do to me. This is the world, endlessly.

Years later, I'd visit Sinead in Ireland. We'd travel around the country and Sinead would give me a gift, a drink coaster with the Phelan family crest on it.

"O'Phelan means of the wolf in Gaelic," she'd say and pat my hand.

The coaster was made of cork. The crest had a deer head on top, a diamond pattern on the shield. I thought I should feel something profound, holding this link to my past, but I didn't. Years later, I'd give the coaster to my birth brother, who planned to get a tattoo of the shield. I don't know if he did, because we're not family, not really.

Family means the people who raised and loved you, and who you raise and love. Friends, too. But blood. That's easy, and not what they say it means in the movies.

***

Once, back in New York, Sinead and I had our palms read by a woman in the East Village. The palm reader's studio was all done up in red velvet. She wore bangles and gauze. She told Sinead, "You long for home."

She told me, "There are lines we're born with, and lines we make for ourselves."

The first line, the one I was born with, was so faint I had to scrunch my palm to see it. Then the palm reader charged me $50, cash.

***

I stayed in Ireland for two weeks, a visitor, a tourist. Everywhere Sinead and I would go, we'd play a game Sinead invented called "Spot the American."

Sometimes it was easy—green t-shirt, tennis shoes, bag full of postcards. One thing I noticed—Americans take up a lot of space. We sprawl. We come from a big country, where we're not used to holding anything, our opinions, even our arms and legs, in. Our body language is open, as if we can absorb the whole world.

By the time we got to Belfast, that sad and troubled place, I'd order our drinks and food because Sinead worried about her accent. Our game was trickier.

We played until finally, in one pub, the only American to spot was me.

Kurt Cobain Knew Nothing About Love

I wanted the giant heart-shaped box, like the one in the Nirvana song but not. Forget roses, stuffed bears, those smaller, more civilized Belgian chocolates in boxes bedazzled with golden ribbons. I wanted chocolate in a box the size of a ham. I wanted a Super-Size-Me box that would have to be strapped into a passenger seat and protected by an airbag.

I wanted a heart that could double as a soapbox my beloved would stand on as he wailed to the world, "Because I love you this much!"

And I got one on Valentine's Day years ago.

I was living in New York then, working as a flight attendant. I'd been dating Diego for a while. We didn't like each other much, but it worked. It worked the way things work when the person next to you on the bus doesn't smell like moldy broccoli or talk to his sandwich. It worked the way two strangers, somewhat attracted to each other, agree to split the rent on a rent-controlled apartment in Queens.

I was away a lot. Diego was a cop and often on duty when I was home. He looked like an action figure in his uniform. We both liked to travel and I had flight benefits. I got a Police Benevolent Association card that helped me get out of parking tickets and someone to call when a roach cuddled my toothbrush. Diego had someone who could take him to Spain on the cheap and make meatballs on the toy-sized stove in his/our apartment.

"I like our arrangement," Diego would say, as if our lives were a bunch of carnations, tacky and bound together out of obligation or necessity, a gesture.

***

I'm not sure when I became obsessed with the big Valentine's heart box, but size-wise it probably had something to do with the box of chocolates my father would bring home from work every Christmas.

My father worked in a tool shop in Wall, PA. His bosses, like most bosses, hated workers, but every Christmas, they'd cough up a hairball of decency and give everyone a four-pound box of chocolates.

"It's the least the bastards can do," my father said.

The box was huge, rectangular, with three layers, an office build-ing full of chocolates, each in its own cubicle.

My parents and I would huddle on the couch and watch the eve-ning news or *T.J. Hooker*, my father's favorite cop show starring Captain Kirk, aka William Shatner after he finished his last voy-age on the Starship Enterprise and took up wearing a toupee that should have come with its own disco ball.

I'd sit between my parents with the box of chocolates on my lap, and we'd grapple for the red-foil-wrapped cherries or the last tof-fee crunch.

"Now isn't this nice?" my father, who rarely seemed happy, said, and he meant, I think, the chocolates, but also the three of us together, watching J.T. Kirk as T.J. Hooker clean up his city's mean streets.

My parents fought so much that every sliver of peace felt like a truce, that box of chocolates between us, all those tiny delicious white flags of joy.

***

That Valentine's Day, Diego showed up, awkward as a salesman in the doorway. We'd had a fight the day before, something about ketchup. I was getting dressed for work. I had a three-day trip, with double layovers in Little Rock.

On the romance scale, Arkansas is not Paris, though Arkansas' official gem is the diamond and the state insect is the honeybee, and Little Rock was once home to Bill Clinton, whose love of blowjobs if not romance is legendary, and Arkansas' state instrument is the fiddle and nothing says sexy like a fiddle-round of "Sadie at the Back Door" or "Who Hit Nellie With the Stove Pipe."

Next to our layover hotel, there was a Waffle House with a perpetual sign on the front window that read "Waffles Are For Lovers, $2.99."

The world told me I should be miserable imagining myself alone on Valentine's Day with a stack of heart-shaped waffles and bottomless coffee, but I wasn't.

The prospects seemed mostly a delight.

"Happy Valentine's Day," Diego said. He tried to tuck the heart behind his back.

He had to come through the door sideways, which speaks to both the size of New York rent-controlled apartments and the size of the heart-shaped box. The box tipped and I could hear the chocolates in there, sliding around.

The box was everything I imagined. Huge, velvet-covered, fake-silk lined. The chocolates were not great, waxy, pretty terrible even, but it didn't matter.

There it was, finally. A heart I could drive off in.

"Love you," Diego said.

He kissed the top of my head while he scoped the room in that cop way he had, checking for evidence of who knows what.

Maybe I thought in that moment, in the red glow emanating from a heart bigger than a New York pizza, that we had something.

Probably not.

"Love you, too," I'm sure I said back.

It was more of a wish, a blessing, than any kind of vow.

"You shouldn't have," I said about the heart, which is what people say when they mean "Thank you. This is both nice and disappointing. This is not what I hoped it would be."

When I tried to put the box of chocolates in the fridge to keep them safe from roaches while I was gone, it didn't fit, the way Diego and I never fit.

This is what's often left out of those commercial Valentine's fantasies—the truth that there are two real people involved and the only thing that matters is how two lives can come together, connect, and somehow hold on.

It would take me years to learn the miracle of that.

Diego sighed. He took the heart to his parents' apartment a few floors down, to their slightly bigger fridge. "We'll be waiting for you," he said, about him and the chocolates and the truth about love I'd yet to learn.

While I was on my Waffle House layover, Diego and his brother would pick through the chocolates. They'd eat all the decent ones and leave finger holes in the bottoms of the leftover pieces, all pink and yellow creams.

I have always hated creams.

"Love you," Diego and I said to each other, not "I love you," but "love you."

As in someone, someday, will.

There Never Were Snakes in Ireland

"I'm Irish," my daughter said this morning when she insisted on me dressing her in three layers of green to celebrate St. Patrick's Day.

I had to get her up 15 minutes early to be sure her nails were glittered and painted green and her hair was done up in a green-bedazzled do.

Today, especially, my daughter talks about her other family, the one overseas. It's a romantic notion and my daughter is beautiful and kind and if ever there were smiling Irish eyes worthy of song, she has them.

Still. "You're American," my husband and I say.

We want her to understand that, to feel the pride of that.

"Don't ruin it," she says.

The Irish part of my daughter, the one she likes to cling to, is complicated, and in many ways it's as much an illusion as that thing with St. Patrick and the snakes.

The story goes that Saint Patrick, Ireland's patron saint, drove all the snakes into the sea after they attacked him during his 40-day fast, snakes being evil interrupters of fasts and all things holy. But Ireland is one of the few places on Earth where snakes can't be found in the wild. There are no fossil records of snakes, and Ireland, an island, was covered in ice during the last glacial period, which means it was too cold for snakes since forever.

"Being American is cool, right?" I say, and my daughter says, "I mean *roots*, like where we're really from."

This is an American problem, no? my French friend Constance and fellow flight attendant would say, and roll her lovely European eyes.

I was adopted, given up by an Irish mother and passed to my first-generation American but deeply ethnic Italian and Polish parents. My father-in-law's parents came from Ireland, but neither I nor my daughter knew them.

Maybe it's because I was adopted. Maybe it's because my idea of family and loyalty and personal history can be loaded into a very small and precious box. But the truth is, I want my children to love the identities they were born into, which means I want them to hold on to who they really are, not an idea of a past that has no real hold in their lives.

At my daughter's school, the teachers assign family ancestry projects. The assignments call for photos and artifacts and genetic records. Teachers assigned these same projects to my son and, many years before that, to me. Most times, my adoption and all the unanswered questions about how I came to be don't bother me much. But sometimes, that small emptiness stings.

I do my best to fill the shoeboxes the teachers send home. I add some Irish souvenirs—a Celtic cross woven from straw, a few postcards, a picture of me shivering at the Cliffs of Moher. Tourist stuff. I add pictures of my parents, pictures of my husband's grandparents, recipe cards my mother wrote by hand, and an old St. Jude medal I found in my father's wallet after he died.

"I wish there was more," my daughter says and sighs.

She decorates her box with pictures she pulls from the internet—Galway, Dublin, a cottage with a thatched roof, green rolling hills.

She gets a good grade, I think.

My father, Polish not Irish, loved St. Jude, the patron saint of lost causes. Praying to St. Jude is supposed to bring hope and optimism, both of which my father needed in this life. My daughter, though, overflows with both. Maybe blessings from St. Jude take a while. Maybe they skip generations. Maybe the hope my father prayed for now rains down on the grandchildren he never knew.

An Irish proverb: "You've got to do your own growing, no matter how tall your father was."

"You think too damn much," my father said. "You can't tell your own ass from a hole in the ground."

So okay, maybe my daughter is better off not knowing the unexplainable intricacies of her heritage, none of which can fit in a shoebox.

My daughter's right. All this thinking is ruining the party. And today is supposed to be all about the party—the green beer, shamrock G-strings, the green face paint that will cling to American eyebrows for weeks, the cars parked crooked for miles at the Ancient Order of Hibernians, all those broken bottles strewn on streets everywhere.

"Jesus, Mary and Joseph," my sweet Irish friend Sinead would say, and bless herself with the sign of the cross to ward off all things Irish-American.

Fun fact: In Ireland, the shamrock is sacred, a representation of the holy Trinity, the sign of the cross. A four-leafed clover, which Americans think of as magic and luck, is an aberration. The first St. Patrick's Day parade was held in America, in a Spanish colony of what is now St. Augustine, Florida, in 1601.

"What I am is what I am / Are you what you are or what?" Edie Brickell sang in America back in the 1980s. Edie Brickell had German roots, maybe, but her band was The New Bohemians. Stateless, rootless, free. I loved that song, probably because of my adoption. She made rootlessness sound like a gift.

"Teach me some Irish," my daughter, whose name is my birth name, old Irish meaning "of the wolf," said this morning.

I know a couple words in Gaelic, in Irish, not from family, but from Sinead and other friends and from working for the airlines and flying in and out of Shannon and Dublin for years.

I teach my daughter "craic." Fun. I teach her "slainte." Health. I teach her "firinne." Truth. I say the words like they're a universal language, bohemian wishes, which of course they are.

On this St. Patrick's Day, I bend down to adjust my daughter's emerald headband before she heads out to the bus stop. Her blonde curls tumble to her shoulders. She takes my face in her sweet hands and says, "Look. My eyes are green, like yours."

I kiss her three times, one on each cheek, once on the lips. "For luck," she says and will go on saying. I watch her walk to the bus stop where all the other neighborhood kids are dressed in green, too.

Everyone looks like everyone.

That night, I and the other parents will use the holiday to drink and toast St. Patrick, the great exterminator, and believe whatever we want.

Pick Yourself Up Off the Ground

One mid-pandemic day, because I love my daughter and because I have what my mother said is the common sense of a doorknob, I found myself sprawled on a tennis court trying not to pass out.

I'd never broken a bone before, mostly because I'm not athletic. The only sport I've ever been competent at is tennis, though my high school tennis coach, a middle-aged man built like a pork chop but a gazelle on the court, would disagree.

This is not about tennis.

Phelan and I decided to take up roller skating during the pandemic, even though all the rinks were shuttered, because we could do it outside.

I prided myself on my skate skills, forged in 20th-century Pittsburgh, those decades of pink-satin bomber jackets, sweaty-palmed couple's skates, the all-skate that welcomed all of us back to the floor, and the dreaded limbo. I was excited to show off for my daughter.

Phe was excited to get a hot pair of skates like ones she saw on TikTok.

As you read this, I will be in the final year of my 50s. I should not dance on wheels or use abbreviations like *holo* or know who's rolling on TikTok. But such is middle-aged parenting.

"I don't want kids to think you have an old woman for a mother," my mother, who adopted me when she was 40, would say.

My mother dyed her hair until she was 70. She wore lipstick, a forever-young shade called Flamingo Pink.

"Don't let yourself go," she'd say about appearances, and I'd say, "Go where?"

I was an only child. For years my mother was my playmate. We played badminton and dressed in matching cat costumes for Halloween. She was Big Pussy. I was Little Pussy. My mother would put notes in my school lunch box. She'd address the notes to "Little Pussy." She'd sign the notes "Love, Big Pussy." This did not play well in the St. Regis Elementary School cafeteria, where bully Mark Capozzetti and his sidekick Bill Ondelowich would swipe said notes and recite them aloud in voices that sounded like Meow Meow Pussycat from "Mister Rogers Neighborhood" if poor Meow Meow had a two-pack-a-day cigarette habit and some understanding of street porn.

"Be sensible," my mother, a nurse who knew nothing about street porn but understood the middle-life dangers of roller skates and other wheeled things, would say.

I was 36 when I had my son, 40 when I had Phe. Sometimes I'm self-conscious about my late start at parenting and I worry how my kids feel about it.

"I don't want you to die!" Phe said years ago. We were having Boston Market mac and cheese, her favorite. We hadn't been talking about mortality. I kissed my daughter, wiped her sudden tears, and assured her I could never die and leave behind such delicious mac and cheese. I made a big deal of stuffing my mouth full to bulging.

"Abbondanza!" my mother would toast at New Year's.

To abundance.

An abundant life.

***

Growing up, I worried my parents would die at any second, so I told them I loved them a lot.

How's the weather? I love you.
Pass the salt, please, I love you.

I wanted "I love you" to be the last thing they heard before they died.

"So creepy," my mother said, and figured it had something to do with my adoption.

It could have. My mother was right about a lot of things.

But back to the skates.

One perfect, blue-skied day, my daughter—sick of online everything—slumped and sighed.

"Can't we do *something?*"

She stretched those two syllables for miles.

Phelan's skates sat in a corner, all siren-song and longing. I had a friend who was a yogi, who was also a rollerskater, and my yogi friend sometimes took her skates for a spin on tennis courts. There was a tennis court nearby—cracked asphalt, nets that seemed gnawed by sharks, mostly abandoned.

So Phe and I packed our skates and a portable speaker. I made a playlist—The Gap Band, the Bee Gees. If you grew up in the '70s and '80s, you know.

The tennis courts were, as expected, empty.

The Gap Band dropped a bomb. The Bee Gees stayed alive.

Phe clung to the fence, then found her skate legs.

I did, too. I did one lap, then another. I felt graceful, skating to memories—my first French kiss, raspberry Icee on my tongue, that swoosh of satin, the possibility of possibility.

Then I hit a crack. And went down hard. The pain in my wrist was slow, then not. I looked at Phe, wheeling around the court. I didn't want to ruin things. I told her to keep skating.

I told her I'd be fine.

***

It's been two years now. The metal plate in my arm, I know from X-rays, is the size of a serving fork. A friend reminded me that, when I'm cremated, the plate will be left simmering in the ashes.

It's such a big piece of metal. Something worth saving, maybe.

"So. Creepy," my mother would say.

When my mother died, I found wadded-up tissues in her make-up drawer, imprints of her pink kisses on them. Something worth saving. I wish I had.

***

I love my daughter. I want to believe we will go on forever, which may be why I recently decided to unearth our skates and head to Eden Park in East McKeesport, my first roller rink, my daughter's first roller rink. Inside the Eden Park entrance there are signs: "Skate at Your Own Risk." "Insurance DOES NOT Cover Injury."

Upstairs, the rink looks the same. A birthday party is going down. Kids trying to cha-cha slide, hollow-eyed parents trying to hold them up like lifeguards doing their best to not drown with the drowning.

I lace my skates, stand up, and hold on to whatever I can. Phelan stays behind me, saying encouraging things like, "You've got this, sweetie," and "You're doing great, sweetie!"

At some point in this living, parents and children switch places, but it's too soon for that. Still, the way my daughter calls me sweetie hits my heart.

My knees wobble but soon I'm flying, dodging downed kids, a human pinball zigging this way and that. When we take a break, Phelan says, "I saw you! You looked young, like another version of yourself."

It's simple magic.

"You go around in a circle and forget your troubles," says Sherri Mellon, 50, whose family has owned Eden Park for decades. "You become a child again. You feel free. Where else can you find that now?"

Phe is 18. She does a few laps. I sit and watch and try to freeze this moment for when I'll need it later. This is, of course, about time, its strange and terrible and lovely passing.

I start to unlace my skates, but then the first notes of the Village People's "YMCA" come on. I lace back up. I'm ready to make my arms into a Y. I'm ready to dance with wheels on my feet.

Then I go down hard.

Phe shouts, "Mom, no!"

I'm flat on my butt.

A group of birthday kids gathers around. One girl, hands on her cheeks, gasps.

I'm fine. I am. I get up. Even though I'll feel it later, I go around, side by side with my almost-grown daughter, laughing, our arms over our heads spelling out letters to a song we both will always know by heart.

Love Saves the Day

"I love you!" my daughter Phelan yells at the woman in the bath aisle at Target. Phelan is four. She's in the cart and bundled in her down jacket and fuzzy scarf. It's February. Outside it's snowing and the snowflakes have melted into her hair. This makes her hair curl, and her blonde pigtails bounce like springs. She dangles one fluffy arm over the side of the cart and waves like a beauty queen.

"I love you!" she yells again, louder, and this time the woman looks up from the bathmats she's holding, two heavy slices of lime green shag, and seems confused.

I came in with a list—double-A batteries, socks, Star Wars boxer shorts for my son Locklin, Phelan's brother, who opted out of this trip so he could go on playing "Battalion Wars II" on his Wii.

"It's not real," Locklin tells me, because he knows I don't like war games.

Sometimes when he catches me watching the news, he'll put his 8-year-old hand on my back and say, "Mom, lighten up. You worry too much."

Maybe he's just repeating lines he's learned from TV. Maybe it's more. These days, there are so many things to worry about—wars, politics, the way my son with his serious green eyes is too much like me.

But my list. I had it in my pocket and had to keep reminding myself to check it. Target confuses me the way Vegas casinos confuse me. There's something about the lights. In Vegas, I go into casinos at night and when I come out it's morning. In Target, I go in with a list that says batteries, socks and boxers, and come out with a bookshelf, a lava lamp, and 30 rolls of toilet paper.

Phelan gets distracted, too. Target has toys and dollar bins and pop-up books. It has hot dogs and Slurpees. Her favorite aisle, though, is the greeting card section. She loves cards, especially the musical kind that play cheesy hits from the '70s and '80s. These are the kind of cards my daughter calls "invitations." She thinks they're magic.

On this day there are Valentine's Day displays—the usual heart-shaped cards and cards featuring sad-eyed puppies and nuns. There are cards with cartoon cows on them and, for cynics, cards with pictures of dead and stomped-on roses. When we came to the card aisle, Phelan bounced and pointed and I forgot about my list and pulled up next to a row of cards that looked like half-eaten boxes of chocolates.

Phelan plucked a card and opened it.

"I love you!" it yelled.

She laughed. She squealed. She closed the card. She opened it again.

"I love you!" it yelled.

She held the card up over her head and waved it. She brought it back down and kissed it.

She closed the card.

She opened it.

She shook it like she was waiting for something, fairies maybe, to tumble out.

She closed the card and opened it again and this time, she yelled back, "I love you!"

I put the card back on the shelf, but Phelan couldn't help herself.

"I love you," she yelled to the slit-mouthed security guard checking receipts, to the sad couple with their basket of air fresheners, to the flop-haired kid in Digital Cameras.

"Shh," I said at first, but then I gave up and let myself enjoy my daughter's rubber-ball voice bouncing off everything and everyone it touched.

"I love you," she yelled to the woman at the concession stand where the wrinkled hot dogs lolled around like tanorexic sunbathers.

"I love you," she yelled to the red-vested manager price-checking tennis shoes, and now, to this woman in the brown tweed coat, her arms laden down with bathmats.

Everyone else had been at a distance, but this woman is close. I'm afraid Phelan might reach out and try to touch her. The woman stares as we push past. She doesn't smile or laugh. She seems, maybe, horrified that I've let my daughter act out like this, and she may be right.

Maybe I should have stopped it.

I look past the woman and half-smile as if to say sorry.

***

Back home, my son is blowing things up with his digital Terror Tanks. The game's soundtrack plays Taps over a smoking battle-field. Here in a store called Target, my daughter's face is flushed with misplaced joy. I feel the pull of the world, what's right and good, what I can change and what I can't.

My son's right, I know. I need to lighten up. But like my daughter and her boundless joy, I can't help it. I push Phelan faster and we turn into the next aisle. Plastic shower curtains covered with Captain America and angelfish. Toothbrush holders shaped like cities. And towels. So many towels. I reach into my pocket for my list. Batteries, socks. All around us, there's a rainbow of fluff and color, the promise of what won't save us—three shades of purple, bubblegum pinks, blues if you want.

I'm touching them, the blues, when I hear a voice from one aisle over. It's the woman with the bathmats. She doesn't quite yell, but she says it loud enough to feel it.

"Love you, too."

Sometimes the world can change, just like that.

Under these bright and almost beautiful lights, for a few minutes at least, I believe, like my daughter believes, in everything good.

A Christmas Season in Flour

I'm in the kitchen. Phelan, my 4-year-old daughter, is in the dining room. I'm mixing dough. Phelan has opened a bag of flour the size of a ham. I don't know this. I should.

I hear her yell, "Snow, snow, snow!"

I hear, "It's winter!"

I hear, "Snowball!"

I've been looking out the kitchen window as the mixer whirs away.

Whenever I bake, I think about my mother. The day is sunny, snowflake-free. There's a space between the time I hear something and the moment I figure out what it means.

"Slippy," my daughter, fluent in Pittsburghese, says. "Cold."

Flour is everywhere, in her hair, in the stereo, in her shoes. Later I'll find flour in her underwear and flour in her socks. But right now, she smiles up at me, flour stuck like snowflakes in her eyelashes, smudged on her pink cheeks, caught in the blonde pigtails that stick out like antennae.

"Look at me," she says. "I'm baking."

***

Every year around the holidays, my husband—who hates chaos, who organizes our house—flees. He goes to a bar and drinks, and the kids and I make a lovely mess. For my daughter, it's flour. My son, Locklin, 7, has moved on to dough. Dough makes great quicksand for his toy soldiers. Dough makes a good mustache. Dough sticks to his sister's butt. The kids have their own rolling pins. They help measure sugar and cinnamon. Phelan gets distracted and gets a bowl, pours herself a nice cinnamon-sugar mix and eats it with a spoon.

When I was growing up, I didn't get to bake with my mother much. It made her nervous. "I don't like people in my kitchen," she'd say as she anchored a childproof gate between the kitchen and dining room. She said the gate was "to keep the dog out."

The dog, a sensitive poodle named Tina II, and I would sit outside the gate and watch my mother break eggs with one hand and toss the shells into the trash in one fluid motion, like a magic trick. She'd turn on the easy-listening station and hum and glide from refrigerator to counter and back. My sad mother the magician. My lonely mother the dancer. How had this happened? The dog and I sulked and waited until my mother passed a peace offering—batter-covered beaters, one for me, one for the dog—over the gate.

I know now that my mother loved the solitary time baking gave her. It offered an excuse to detach from the world, from the dog and my father and me, and make something her own. It's what I do when I write, when I close my office door and leave my children and husband on the other side.

"A room of one's own," Virginia Woolf called it. Space to make something beautiful.

When I did get to bake with my mother, we made handprint sugar cookies. My job was to put my hands onto the rolled-out dough and hold still. Real baking—the breads, nut rolls, all the family traditions—my mother did alone. It wasn't until after my son was born, a few years before she died, that my mother finally gave in and decided to teach me.

I'd like to say I was a natural, that all those years of watching paid off, but it's not true. Our first lesson, bread, was a disaster.

***

My mother told me to be at her house at 5 a.m. Mornings make me want to weep. I was late, 5:15, and I looked a mess. My mother wasn't happy. Her gray hair was curled. She had on her favorite track suit, purple velour with gold piping at the cuffs, and was wearing tennis shoes. She looked like she'd been waiting for hours.

"What's the matter with you?" she said. "You have to start bread early."

I didn't know what that meant. I also didn't know what she meant when she said, "Bread is serious business. Bread is no joke."

I laughed during my lesson, my forearms buried in a swamp of sticky dough. My mother whacked me on the arm with her wooden spoon.

"Look," she said. "Do you want to learn or not?"

She picked up her bowl of dough and pulled it to her belly like a child. She dipped one arm in and lifted the dough up and over, whipping more than kneading, the muscles in her arm flexed and solid and nowhere near 70 years old.

"This is how you do it," she said. "You have to work it. You have to mean it."

My mother talked about yeast and bread as living things, things to conquer, things you could kill if you weren't careful. She didn't use measuring cups and spoons. "You just know," she said, her hands measuring flour and sugar by weight, by how it moved through her fingers. "You can feel it."

My mother's been dead for years now. I still feel the weight of that.

"You need to learn how to do this," she said. "Because when I die, then what?"

***

In the dining room, my daughter helps me spread more flour on the table. We laugh and smooth out the mounds until there's a dusting.

"Snow," she says. "Snow snow snow snow snow."

I separate the dough into bowls, one for each of us. My son rolls his into tiny balls. He launches them like cannonballs with his thumb.

"Pow," he says. "Bang."

"Snowball," my daughter says.

My mother wouldn't appreciate our approach, but within a few hours the house fills with smells I remember from childhood, and I lay the golden loaves onto racks to cool.

When my husband comes home, we have the flour under control. My daughter's face is scrubbed and I've picked the dough out of my son's hair.

"Look," Phelan says as she takes her father by the hand to show him what we've made. "Isn't it beautiful?"

Soft

My daughter Phelan weeps every New Year's Eve. It started when she was four years old. Decked out in party hats that cut lines into our cheeks, we watched Anderson Cooper and Kathy Griffin pretend-flirt as the ball started to fall like a small planet over Times Square.

Phelan leaned into me and her body stiffened like she was bracing for impact. When everyone yelled "Happy New Year!" and fireworks and confetti filled the TV screen, Phelan buried her face in my hair. She flung herself at her father's chest and swatted her brother. She dropped to the floor, boneless, inconsolable, and we had no idea why.

"Goodbye, goodbye," she cried.

"I miss the good old days," she said later, and I said, "You're 4, sweetie."

My daughter was born with a beautiful sense of nostalgia.

"Old soul," my friend Tonya says.

Tonya runs a yoga studio filled with Buddha statues and incense, dried flowers and velvety drapes in our rusty mill town of Trafford. The studio used to be Mel's Barber Shop. The Westmoreland Ghost Hunters occasionally stop by, believing Mel, who played stand-up bass, haunts the place.

When she's alone at night, Tonya hears music. She knows old souls. I think she might, like my daughter, be one. The best people are. Tonya hears her dead grandparents. She knows we all struggle.

When we replaced the floor in our kitchen, Phelan, who was 7 then, wept over that, too. She threw herself onto the sticky yellowed tiles that had been in place since the 1970s.

"Goodbye, floor," she said, like she was losing a friend.

I tried to pick her up. The floor was not only old, but gross. Desiccated Cheerios, bits of old toast and cookie crumbs stuck in her long blonde curls.

I said, "Sweetheart, what's wrong? You'll love the new floor. You can slide across it in your socks. It'll be like ice skating."

"Really?" she said and tried to smile.

Then she wept again.

The same thing happened when we tried to replace the stained carpet in her bedroom, when we tried to paint her walls, and when our minivan died.

Phelan was 8 when we bought a lime-green replacement Kia.

"Goodbye, van," she said. "We had some good times."

Lime green was her favorite color that year. It showed up in every picture she drew.

"Your brother threw up in that van all the time," I said.

The car salesman, rubbing his comb-over, tried to console my daughter. He gave her a lollipop. He gave her a balloon. Phelan thanked him and kept crying.

"What's wrong with that kid?" another salesman said.

***

When I was a child, I cried a lot.

My mother, annoyed and worried, bought a book called *Cry-Baby Duck* and read it to me at bedtime. Children's books have morals, and this one wanted me to toughen up.

"Cry-baby duck," my mother would say whenever I was upset. "Let's have a pity party, one two three, awwww."

The duck in that story cried because he wanted to be bigger, prettier, less duck-ish. The duck in that story cried whenever he didn't get his way. None of these were the reasons I cried, and my mother knew that.

"You and your feelings," she said, like feelings made her itchy. "Grow a thicker skin already."

A few years ago, when Phelan was 10, we found a copy of *Cry-Baby Duck* and read it together. When we were done, Phelan looked stunned.

"What kind of monster reads a book like that to a child?" she said.

Sometimes I worry my daughter is too sensitive. Sometimes I wish I could find armor to protect her from the loss that will come and keep coming. My mother wasn't being cruel. She was afraid. She was afraid I wouldn't stop crying. When I worry about Phelan, I try to remember that her capacity for tears is matched only by her capacity for joy.

One day, years ago, her brother Locklin caught her spinning and dancing in the kitchen.

"Life isn't all daisies and roses, you know," Locklin said.

My practical son. My beautiful serious boy.

Phelan kept spinning.

She laughed and said, "Who's Daisy?"

Locklin's first words were "duck" and "light."

"Duck!" my son would yell when we drove under an overpass. "Light!" he'd yell when he was afraid at night. For my son, language was a way of controlling his world. He wanted safety—"duck!" "light!"—most of all.

My son is so much like me.

But my daughter?

Her first word was "abre," Spanish for "open." When she said it, she held her arms wide, reaching out of her crib, like she wanted to take the whole world in.

"Be soft," Kurt Vonnegut Jr. said. "Do not let the world make you hard."

My daughter is 13 now, embarrassed by her big feelings, I think. Life feels harder and crueler every day. Just turn on the news. And still.

In October, Phelan and I visited Times Square. She looked up at the Toshiba tower, the ball tucked safely in place. She looked around, the lights on Broadway, the smiling people taking pictures.

"It's all too beautiful," she said about New York, about the world.

Portrait of a Young Artist in Suburbia

My daughter wears a frog hat to drum lessons. The hat has felt eyes that google on top of her head. It has legs for ear flaps, a tongue for a visor, and chin straps that look like a lilypad and lotus.

"Stylin,'" her teacher Mike says, "a real drummer," and pats Phelan right between her amphibian eyes.

Mike looks like Billie Joe Armstrong from Green Day—black spiked hair, smudged eyeliner, mellow rock swagger. He's kind and patient and says cool with two syllables.

Phelan is 8 now. She is blonde and green-eyed and the nicest person I know. She also questions a lot of things. Last year at the school talent show, she did a tough-guy drum solo, Survivor's "Eye of the Tiger." She wore a pink skirt and sequined top. Her glittered shoes lit up like an emergency whenever she took a step.

My daughter confuses people, which confuses her, which worries me.

"I like girl things and boy things," she tells me, like she's confessing something, like she wants me to give her some penance to do.

"You're perfect," I say. "Always be yourself."

"Always be yourself," she repeats to her older brother when he's embarrassed by her abundant joy and questionable fashion sense.

My son is 12. It's a tough age made worse because he worries too much about what other people think. When he was very young, around four, he'd do stand-up routines in our basement.

He had a catchphrase—"And I threw up... two times"—that could make adults howl.

Then something happened. I don't know what.

A year passed, maybe two.

He stopped telling jokes. He stayed away from microphones. At the playground, he'd stand like an accountant, hands in pockets, and watch the other kids play before he'd join in.

"Don't smile too much. Stand back. Be cool," he tells his sister now, his advice on being popular.

"I'm my own person," she says, and whacks him with a drumstick.

It's not good for my daughter to whack her brother with a drumstick. She gets in trouble for this. Her dad says, "Hey," and, "Stop that," and, "Be sweet." I say "gentle now" and mean everybody. Still, I hope she'll find some way to go on holding the world off. I hope my son will find his way back.

In my kids' school, there are anti-bullying signs everywhere. The signs have inspirational messages. "Everyone is Special." "You're Perfect the Way You Are." "Difference is Beautiful." "Nothing is Better Than Being Yourself."

But being yourself costs, especially when you're 8 like my daughter, especially when mean girls are rising up, all preen and snicker, hips like switchblades jutted out.

People say kids are naturally mean, but I think meanness is a learned thing.

Those anti-bullying signs are earnest. My kids' school is wonderful. We live in the suburbs and our school district is one of the best around. But in our district, there are subdivisions with regal names, pre-fab houses with coordinated siding and matching mailboxes. All the homes look the same, eggs in a carton. There's a push, I think, for all the people to be the same, too—paperweights in their own little boxes, scissors with blunted tips.

"We're very particular about who we let move in here," one woman from a nearby subdivision said recently.

I don't know who she meant by "we" or who exactly fit her criteria. Or maybe I do know and it's too awful to think about.

Difference is scary. If it can be gated off, if it can be shrunken down into something manageable, a petri dish, life can seem easier to navigate. This doesn't excuse anything.

"Do you know your enemy?" Green Day's Billie Joe Armstrong wants to know.

*****

My family lives in the house I grew up in, close to the cluster of subdivisions this woman was talking about. Our house has been here for 40 years, but some days I feel like an outsider, even though most of our neighbors are sweet, the kind of people who help in an emergency. They're the kind of people who bring casseroles and who, if they see your trash can rolling down the street, will stop, pick it up, and deliver it back where it belongs.

But my husband and I are writers, which makes us seem a little odd. We don't have expensive furniture. We do have a lot of books. We have a lot of paintings and music, too. We're what my mother would have called "arty." She would not have meant this as a compliment. My son constantly reminds us we live in a house and not an art gallery.

"Can't we please be normal?" he says.

"Do you collect books?" a neighbor asks.

"I know why you have so many books," one of my daughter's friends says. "So people will think you don't watch TV."

"Books, huh?" one of my son's friends says.

Yes, I say. That's right.

"And you actually read them?" he says, like books are a virus that might be contagious.

"Be yourself," I tell my daughter, even though most days I'm a hypocrite, terrified of being found out.

About writing, the great Harry Crews once said, "World don't want you to do that. World wants you to go to the zoo and eat cotton candy, preferably seven days a week."

I want my children to be their own beautiful selves.

I also want the world to go easy on them.

I'm not sure it's possible to have both.

If meanness is learned, other things are learned, too. Contradiction, for instance.

When I was growing up, subdivision wasn't a word people used.

We had our street, neighborhood, block. I think about that word now, subdivision, the root of it. The division of a larger division. The act of dividing again and again.

"Maybe I should try cheering," my daughter says when she worries about fitting in. "Maybe I should get an American Girl doll."

But I'm thankful she hasn't followed up on any of that.

She sings and plays softball and every Thursday, she straps on her frog hat and does her drum lessons with Mike. Right now they're working from a book called *The Rock and Roll Bible*.

"It's a foundation," Mike tells Phelan. "Once you learn your system, you're solid. You can do anything."

They count together, one-e-and-a-two-e-and-a, and my pretty blonde daughter bangs out a beat like Charlie Watts. On her head, the frog eyes bob. When she plays, she's happy, but serious, too. She wants to get this right. The thing about frogs is they're as comfortable on land as in water. Lotuses are rooted and floating all at once.

"The test of a first-rate intelligence is the ability to hold two opposing ideas in mind at the same time." F. Scott Fitzgerald said that.

"Mom, you worry too much. We're fine," my son says.

I watch my daughter drum, her whole body moving, connected, one undivided lovely self, and I believe my sweet son. We're fine.

We are and will be fine.

In Here, Life is Beautiful

The butterfly kit I'd ordered came with six caterpillars. They arrived in what looked like Tupperware. I couldn't believe they survived the trip.

"Are they OK?" my daughter, Phelan, said. She tried not to sound concerned as she jiggled the container.

The caterpillars were spindly, barely moving.

"I'm sure they're fine," I said, but the kit had been on sale, 40% off.

"We guarantee at least three caterpillars to become happy adult butterflies!" the description said.

Phelan asked, "How do they know they'll be happy?" Her green eyes were serious, a scientist weighing fact from opinion.

***

The butterflies were for a middle school project. Phelan was having a hard time then, though she acted happy and brave.

"Such a joy," her teachers wrote on her report cards.

"You are my heart," I'd say to my daughter.

What terrible pressure to put on someone, a line deserving an apology.

About the butterflies' feelings, I said, "Caterpillars probably want wings more than anything. Wings make them happy. Probably."

***

Middle school—that vicious gauntlet of periods and breasts, bullies and their even-nastier mothers in bedazzled designer jeans.

Once, on the school bus, my daughter sat with a kid who lived in a fancier house. The kid's mom boarded the bus and moved her daughter to another seat, next to a child whose parents made more money and banned "SpongeBob SquarePants."

Many mothers in our neighborhood thought "SpongeBob" was a bad influence, all that unrestrained joy. They thought Patrick Star was gay because—pink starfish?

I should have said something to the mother, to the bus driver, but I was confused. Could an adult be that cruel to a child?

I wanted to think not.

The bus drove off. My daughter looked away, not blowing her usual kisses.

"If you thought you saw me crying, you didn't," my daughter said later.

It hurts even now to write this.

No wonder the weight of growing up makes many girls slump, as if they could fold their shoulders in like wings, something to disappear beneath.

***

"Pull your shoulders back," my mother said whenever she caught me slouching.

"Pull your shoulders back," I tell my daughter, because we all become our mothers, no matter what.

I tell my daughter to pull up, like an airplane, to keep her from crashing, to save her from the gravity of the world.

***

"There is no coming to consciousness without pain," Carl Jung said. Lately I've been re-reading Jung's ideas about life's stages. "Who looks outside, dreams," Jung said.

As I write this, Phelan is in her dream time, her first year at college. My daughter is, Jung would say, becoming. She's turning outward, studying acting at a conservatory in Virginia. She says she feels most alive on stage—all that early awkwardness vanished, pushed away like the vegetables she still refuses to eat.

Twice my daughter performed in drag, something that would make those *SpongeBob*-fearing mothers gasp. Phelan loves glittery makeup and sequined gowns. She loves feather boas and does a great Liza Minnelli as Sally Bowles in *Cabaret*.

"I feel like myself, only bigger," Phelan says about drag, that ancient art created when only men could become actors. In her dorm, a poster of Liza beams behind Phelan's bed like a beacon.

Jung said all of life is a journey toward the Self, the discovery of who we truly are.

***

It's a beautiful thing to see my daughter perform, shoulders back, arms thrown wide, even as I feel myself turning inward.

"Who looks inside, awakes," Jung said about this sunset, middle-aged stage of life.

My daughter's absence feels bigger than I thought it would. Soon she'll come home for Thanksgiving. I'll make macaroni and cheese. I'll keep all the vegetables away. But I know my daughter will be changed, and I'll be changed, and we'll have to find new ways to move forward together.

"We cannot change anything until we accept it," Jung said.

***

For now, I've kept Phelan's bedroom door closed. Sometimes I forget and think she's in there. I have to stop myself from knocking, wanting to share a silly video—birds swearing, our favorite —or just plop on her bed to gab and plan our next adventure.

For a while after my mother died, I left the lights on in her house. When I'd drive by, I'd see the lights and let myself believe she was alive in there, watching reruns of *The Golden Girls* and eating the Cheetos her doctors forbade.

***

And then one day I turned off the lights. And then one day, I erased my mother's voice from my voicemail, though sometimes I can still hear her. Losing my mother is not the same as my daughter going off to college, I know, but I feel the losses piling up.

"There is no coming to consciousness without pain," Jung said. That unfortunate truth of being alive.

I wouldn't call what I'm feeling a crisis. I have work I love. I have grown children I love and a husband who rubs my feet when they hurt. My feet always hurt. I teach. I write. I read. I have what's called purpose.

***

And yet.

"Leave your troubles outside!" the master of ceremonies in *Cabaret* says. "Life is disappointing? Forget it!"

Life is a cabaret, old chum.

Only five of those caterpillars hatched at first. The sixth chrysalis fell to the bottom of the cage. One of the other butterflies stayed next to it and kept watch until it opened, despite the odds.

***

"I knew he'd be okay," Phelan said.

***

The day we set the butterflies free, Phelan and I watched them fly off. The weather report wasn't great. I worried we'd set them free to die. But a butterfly's lifespan is a sketchy thing—two weeks to nine months to a year.

"The sole purpose of human existence is to kindle a light in the darkness," Jung wrote in an article for *The Atlantic* in 1962.

"They look happy," my daughter said, and I said, "They do."

Boy Crazy, or Sex and Death from
Kindergarten to Grade Eight

1.

Subject: Dale Miller, Kindergarten

Attributes: Blonde. Built like a pork chop. Proximity a plus—mat next to mine at nap time. Comes complete with new box of crayons (the big box with built-in sharpener and four shades of green—e.g. worldly).

Love Story: Shares his Snack Pack pudding (double chocolate) and gives me the pull top as a ring and stows away on my bus the first day of school because he says I am beautiful like a bride and we are married by Snack Pack forever and ever.

Feeling: I do not agree or disagree to the marriage thing. The Snack Pack pull-top cuts my pinkie finger. First understanding of romantic ambivalence.

Outcome: Dale's mother calls the police because she thinks he's been kidnapped. First lesson about white vans.

2.

Subject: Mark Sundberg, First Grade

Attributes: Blonde. Very pale. Possibly borderline albinism. No eyelashes. Has to stay inside during recess because of sun = sensitive/exotic. Built like a wacky waving inflatable arm-flailing tube man, the kind found outside used car dealerships and Wal-Mart grand openings.

Love Story: Gives me spoon ring he wins from gumball machine. Win = lucky, but then I realize the machine is full of spoon rings. The ring turns my finger green and I think my finger will fall off and I'll be four fingered forever and no one will ever love me again because I won't have a finger to put a ring on and I will die alone or become a nun like Sister Lucilla, aka Sister Lucifer, evil incarnate in a frayed yellow girdle, but even Sister Lucilla wears a ring on her ring finger because she's married to Jesus and has all ten craggy fingers.

Feeling: Rings = love, no matter how green a finger turns. (See Snack Pack pull tab, etc.)

Outcome: Finger does not fall off. My mother paints the ring with clear nail polish and I continue wearing it. First lesson in devotion. Also, first lesson in gangrene and the power of precious metals to stave off death. Also, first lesson in using a calculator to swear. Punch in 1134, turn the calculator upside down and it does your swearing for you. As in, Sister Lucifer, go to hell and take your Jesus ring with you.

3.

Subject: RIP Mark Sundberg, Second Grade

Attributes: Mark's parents split up and he moves away. While he is absent, I imagine he becomes muscular and tan. He becomes more handsome than any of the Tiger Beat posters on my wall. He is a Tiger Beat poster. He is a Disney hero. He is more handsome than the doctors on TV. He is more handsome than my doctors. He is more handsome than my dad. He is more handsome than Sister Lucifer's Jesus. I will never love anyone else ever again.

Love Story: Before he moves, he gives me another ring he took from his mother's jewelry box. It does not turn my finger green, but I have to give it back when his mother calls my mother.

Feeling: I want to keep the ring.

I want to keep the ring.

I should be allowed to keep the ring.

(See note about devotion above)

Outcome: First lesson in nostalgia and the power of distance. Also, some rings are worth more than other rings.

4. **Subject:** Joey Paola, Third Grade

Attributes: Partner for square dancing class. Almost my height. Red haired. Possibly permed. People call him Measle because he has so many freckles, but I think of him more as a connect-the-dots game. I like Word Search puzzles more but connect-the-dots are okay on placemats and pass the time when you're waiting for your food at Kings Family Restaurant.

Love Story: He isn't afraid to hold my hand in health class when we watch movies about cartoon sperms and eggs. He has sweaty palms. I will forever think palm-sweat = romantic. Also, hay bales and fiddles and anything coming round the mountain.

Feeling: Hand holding is sexy, except when Sister Lucilla catches you and smacks your hands with her ruler and calls you little horn-toad cabbage heads.

Outcome: Joey P. sends me a note where I have to say whether or not I am officially his girlfriend—pick one: yes, no, maybe. I check maybe. He dumps me for Gigi Eathorne, who can't square dance but has great pigtails and a red-checked snappy shirt and will grow up to be a biker.

5.
Subject: Kenny O'Hara, Fifth Grade

Attributes: My first drummer. Red haired. Short with teeth that look like they've been hit with a hammer. Hamster-esque personality. Always moving, legs twitching, air drumming, like he's licked a taser. Never dull.

Love Story: We start a band in my parents' basement. Kenny O is in my parents' basement when I get my period. I don't know it's my period. I think I've crapped myself. I call my mother into the bathroom and show her my underwear and she hands me a pink booklet titled *So You're a Woman Now*.

Feeling: Just no.

Outcome: I break up with Kenny later that week. I figure he must know about the period and I'm not ready for that.

6.
Subject: Ronnie Peduzzi, Sixth Grade

Attributes: Nickname Toofy. Athlete. Chews tobacco (e.g. worldly). Swears (e.g. worldly). Missing front tooth. Lost front tooth when it was embedded in Rocky Minoccucci's head during a pick-up game of basketball.

Love Story: Play Spin the Bottle at a party. When he kisses me, he slips what I think is his tongue but then realize is his fake tooth into my mouth.

Feeling: This is not romantic. This is not even French.

Outcome: There is not enough Scope mouthwash in my parents' bathroom to erase the taste of fake tooth and tobacco spit and shame.

7.
Subject: Randy Blakemore, Seventh Grade

Attributes: My second drummer. Long hair. Three years older. Smells like burnt licorice, though it is probably pot and sweat but I don't know that yet.

Love Story: Write rhyming love poems to Randy, who never notices me except for the one time he tells me I'd be okay if I wore more flannel and Love's Baby Soft. I buy flannel. Lots of flannel. I douse myself in Love's Baby Soft and break out in a rash. I write more poems. Randy falls for Lisa DiGiambattista when she plays guitar barefoot in the school talent show.

Feeling: First lesson in pining and loving from afar. Also, the power of barefoot guitar-playing. Also, what's in Love's Baby Soft that makes it so itchy?

Outcome: Abundance of flannel. An allergic Love's Baby Soft rash that requires a visit to a dermatologist and several cortisone shots.

8.
Subject: Ronnie Peduzzi, Eighth Grade

Attributes: See above.

Love Story: I am preparing for my move to all-girls school because my parents have decided I'm boy crazy. Have second Spin-the-Bottle encounter with Ronnie Peduzzi, who swears this time to keep his tooth in his mouth.

Feeling: It's important to trust in the power of love.

It's important to believe in people. Romance = risk.

Outcome: Toofy lied about the tooth.

Enlightenment in Blue

"I would trade all of my technology for an afternoon with Socrates."
—Steve Jobs, Apple Computer

Six hours into the Zoom classes my university mandates I teach during the pandemic, my body goes upright, then fetal, my shoulders slouch, orphans huddled around the fake fire of the computer screen. My computer is an Apple. Apple computers are supposed to have the best tech.

Remember Plato's "Allegory of the Cave?"

Remember what an apple did to Adam and Eve?

Remember the apple and Snow White?

"I ate civilization," Aldous Huxley wrote in *Brave New World,* "and it poisoned me."

It's what I feel: poisoned.

I pull my spine up and back, up and back.

My right side pings.

***

I love teaching. I love my students. I miss them. Zoom classes feel bloodless, lifeless. Huddling around a computer all day feels bloodless, lifeless. Zoombies, we call each other. Zoom zoom, we say, like we're going somewhere. Funny, right?

Right?

***

Years ago, I did a different kind of work, more body than mind, more world than keyboard. I worked on an airplane, a human swirled with other humans in a giant test tube.

Turbulence was always something. Everything unexpected, everything uncontrolled. Flight seems magical, out-of-body ordinary until it's not. Once, I was thrown mid-flight, a plane hit by lightning, then hit again by lightning. The plane dropped then steadied and I ended up five rows from where I'd been standing.

My back was a mess for a while after that. I saw a chiropractor in New York who cracked my spine so much it started to align itself like typesetting when I stood in the shower. I started thinking of my spine as Scrabble tiles. I started thinking of my spine as a Connect Four game.

That ping in my right side started when I was a flight attendant and now when it surfaces, I think of it as a postcard, the way I think of scars as postcards, my body stamped with time and place and memory—I was here and here and here. Physicality as presence. Physicality as meaning.

Proof of life, maybe.

"Don't you have your own seat in the back?" a passenger on that dropped plane said when I tried to buckle into a seat next to him, afraid for the next drop, and the next. He looked at me like I might be contagious. He looked at me like my own vulnerability might make him vulnerable, too.

***

"Work gives you meaning and purpose," the great Stephen Hawking said, "and life is empty without it."

Stephen Hawking left his wife Jane for his much-younger nurse, who handled the work of caring for Stephen Hawking's body so his brain could go on with its own kind of magic. When the nurse tired of the work Stephen Hawking required, Stephen Hawking went back to Jane, his wife, who handled Stephen Hawking's body so Stephen Hawking's brain could go on with its own kind of work.

I worked in the air, then I worked on the ground until it became a computer screen.

We are all contagious now.

***

I was catering as a side gig when a woman, a judge whose politics were all sunshine and $200 haircuts, started to call me the help, but stopped before she could finish the word.

What came out was hel before she remembered my name, almost.

"Laura," she said, and it sounded almost graceful and elegant, like a bow, like she meant it.

God, I hate that name.

My name is Lori, like the bird.

Lories are tiny, bright-colored. They love sugar. Lories, bird watchers say, are intense personalities, the party people of the avian kingdom. High spirited, high energy. Confetti with wings. Rainbows on meth. Lories love nectar, which means they have mainly liquid poop, which, according to experts, Lories love to shoot great distances.

"They're real assholes," a woman who worked at the Pittsburgh Aviary said. "They're pretty right up until they shit on your head."

***

My New York chiropractor was a tiny man who climbed my back like a spider monkey and pressed his knee into my spine to get it to pop. He had a lovely assistant, a masseuse, blonde, pillow-titted, who'd hook me up to electrodes and rub me down with oils that would heat and keep heating long after the massage was done.

The airline I worked for gave me good insurance, great insurance.

In the event of an incident, the benefits brochures said.

My little New York chiropractor told me stories of all the people he knew who were injured like me, but by elevators.

"Nothing so glamorous," he said, and cracked a section of my spine he could name with a number.

Elevators drop a lot in New York, which is kind of like a plane dropping. Imagine all those New Yorkers, headed to work, all those elevators going up and down all those spines of all those buildings, so many cables loose as rubber bands.

No matter what kind of work you do, maybe, the gravity of the world will hurt.

***

"It will cut," Doug, one of the hosts of a TV show I love says, his catchphrase. The show is *Forged in Fire*, a reality show where people make things—knives, mostly, but also swords and daggers.

I love to watch people make things that matter. I love work that produces something tangible, even if that tangible thing is meant to kill.

Doug from *Forged in Fire* has the sweetest face. When he wields a knife or a sword to test it, he slices through bamboo and rope and bags of money. Sometimes he slices through a dummy made to bleed like a person.

When Doug slices through a dummy made to bleed like a person, he stops and smiles and changes his catchphrase.

"It will kill," he says, and his smile is sweet as a blade of grass.

***

"Because there is a law such as gravity, the universe can and will create itself from nothing," Stephen Hawking said.

"It is not necessary to invoke God to light the blue torch and set the universe going."

Stephen Hawking said that, too.

***

Beyond the occasional catering gig, I do not do the kind of work that makes things that can be tested. I move words around a page, creating worlds out of nothing. I teach online classes to students who sometimes turn their cameras on and sometimes are just black rectangles with names. Some of my students are clever and film themselves on a loop so they seem present, forever and ever, Stephen Hawking's black holes.

When I say I move words on a page, I mean on a computer.

I mean my eyes hurt.

I mean I have special glasses now. They're called Blue Lights.

***

Blue Light Specials—something from diners, way back. Something exciting from Kmart. As a kid, I'd go with my mother to Kmart. I'd get an Icee, cherry flavored, and a soft pretzel. My mother would wait for the Blue Light Special to be announced over a loudspeaker and then we'd rush with the other shoppers toward a blue light that beamed, an alien beacon of mystery and savings, somewhere in the store.

Remember mysteries? Remember surprise? Remember believing in things?

There isn't a Kmart anywhere near where I live now, but I think about it. What people might do to one another during a Blue Light Special. The cheap blue beacon that says, come this way, there's money to be saved, if only you get there in time.

***

"When there's no more room in hell," Peter in the zombie classic *Dawn of the Dead* says, "the dead will walk the earth."

At my computer, I pull my zoombie'd spine straight, shoulders back, flexing where wings might be if I had wings.

About Lories—they are social creatures. They live for the time they can spend outside their cages. Keep a Lori in a cage too long, it will start to self-mutilate.

I flex the muscles in my shoulders, strung tight as piano wires, and try to get my back to crack. I take my hands off the computer keyboard and crack my knuckles even though my mother warned against this. "You'll get man hands," she'd say, but my hands still look pretty much like my hands. Older every day, but still. When I worked the catering gig for the judge, I made sure to do my nails—polished, buffed pink.

When I handed out appetizers, I made sure not to offend.

I love the way sometimes, when I'm fresh, my fingers move over the computer keyboard like a piano, the music of all those words.

When I was flying, we flight attendants were taught to keep our nails nice, and brace our bodies, prepare for the worst, hold our shoulders tight against our jumpseats, hands under thighs, palms up. We kept our hands under our legs to keep them from burning in the event of an incident, which is what we called such things. Our hands, we knew, were important, the tools we'd need to open an emergency exit, to lift and push, to help people.

We wanted, most of all, to help people.

Come this way.

Good exit.

***

"The hel...," the judge with the lovely hideous politics said. She couldn't say the P in help, which is what she called us. The P hurt her tongue, I guess.

Her expensive hairdo looked like a wig.

When someone at the judge's catered party dropped a plastic

fork onto the judge's Persian rug, the entire room froze. When someone at the judge's catered party dropped a plastic fork onto the judge's Persian rug, I got down on my knees with a bottle of club soda and a rag and scrubbed and scrubbed at the spot that wasn't there, but might be there, but wasn't, just in case.

***

In Plato's allegory, Socrates describes a group of people who have been chained to the wall of a cave. They've been there all their lives. These people watch shadows projected on the wall from objects passing in front of a fire that's burning just behind them, though the people never turn around to see it. The people give names to the shadows. The shadows become the people's reality. The people stare and stare at the shadows, which are beautiful, the way they move, and the shadows mesmerize then make the people's eyes hurt a bit, all that play of light and dark.

The enlightened person, Socrates says, will ultimately turn to the real light. The enlightened person will break free from the chains and see light for light. But most people, Socrates says, don't want to leave the cave. They accept the life they're given.

They call it real.

Kindness is Its Own Memory

This story involves bad pantyhose and poor sports reportage, but it also involves the late great Franco Harris—forever famous for his years with the Pittsburgh Steelers and "The Immaculate Reception"—and another link on his chain of good deeds.

Back in the late 1980s, I worked for Penn State—Franco Harris's alma mater. I worked in public relations and sports information, despite knowing almost nothing about sports. My bosses were 1980s power-suit women who saw themselves as mentors for clueless marshmallow neophytes like me.

My bosses taught me a lot of hard lessons: how important it was for women to wear make-up, but not too much make-up; how essential it was for women to smile, but not smile too much. They taught me the power of shoulder pads that could double as oven mitts, the importance of learning to walk in heels that could stand in as weapons in James Bond films, and how kindness is often misunderstood as weakness.

"Ice that crap over," my one boss said about on-the-job feelings.

"Hold the tears for people who care enough to pass the Kleenex," my other boss said, a mantra I think she practiced in mirrors and wrote on Post-It notes she stuck to her fridge.

The 1980s were strange times. When I was hired at Penn State to do Penn State things, pantyhose were required for women. L'eggs pantyhose were favorites, in colors called Suntan and Nude.

They came in plastic eggs, like every new pair was hatching something wonderful.

I forget what my bosses said about pantyhose, but it was understood that naked legs were as off-limits as feelings on the job.

One day, at a golf-outing fundraiser, I had a raging fever. I hardly ever ran a fever, so I was sure I was dying. I was sweaty and woozy and incapable of raising any funds unless the funds I was raising were for my own coffin. This was summer, so the pantyhose I was obliged to wear stuck to my legs like a layer of wax. I plucked at them, trying to get a little air in. My bosses saw me plucking and sweating and were livid. I was an embarrassment and, possibly, a fiscal disaster.

Enter Franco Harris.

Franco—Penn State's star running back and sweetheart. Pittsburgh Steelers' star running back and sweetheart. He must have seen I was close to passing out. He must have seen through the smile I'd pasted on because this was my first real job, and because I wanted to be the kind of woman who was tough enough to smile but not too much, to wear make-up, but not too much, and because I very much did not want to be fired.

Franco stepped between me and one of my bosses.

He said, "Sweetheart, you don't look so good."

I can't remember what I said to him. Everything is a bit fuzzy, fever and all, but kindness is its own memory, folding over an otherwise lost moment like a blanket.

Still, I remember Franco, that lovely huge man, my hometown legend. He took me by the arm, right in front of my boss, who glared but couldn't argue. Franco took me to a car. I think it was a nice car. Black, shiny. He put me in the backseat, where there was a cooler filled with popsicles. Franco was in the healthy popsicle business back then. He told me to eat a popsicle. Maybe two. He told me his driver would take me home. He said not to worry. He'd smooth things over.

"Just get some rest and get better," he said, and in my fever-frazzled memory, Franco winked.

***

Dear former bosses:

I think you meant well.

Thank you for trying.

Even now, my mascara looks like bed bugs running a relay down my cheeks. Blush makes me look like I've inhaled too much helium. My lips are so thin that TikTok make-up tutorials advise sketching new lips, better lips, with lip pencils, which make me look like the Joker but without the murderous gravitas. When I try to walk in heels, I look like Buster Keaton doing a silent-movie stunt. I haven't worn pantyhose for a decade at least, and L'eggs come in boxes now anyway, and what fun is that?

I smile every chance I get. My laugh is loud and sounds a bit crazy, I think. I try to tell the truth because everything else is harder.

Have you read Kurt Vonnegut? I love Kurt Vonnegut, who said there's only one rule in this life, "Be kind, babies." Kurt Vonnegut said people should stay soft and not let the world make them hard. It's good advice. I'm trying to take it.

***

During the years I held my Penn State job, I failed epically.

I cried once, despite not being a crier, in the office of my Penn State Sports Director, who hated me because he discovered how little I knew about sports. I tried to take stats at a basketball game. It didn't go well. "Useless," the Sports Director said, and threw some stats sheets and a pen at me and my tears surprised both of us.

Before Penn State, I worked for the *Erie Daily Times* covering sports, but not really. My editors were my college journalism professors, kind men who thought it might be good to have a young woman covering sports.

Maybe I was a diversity hire in the newsroom, though we didn't have that language back then. My editors were simply kind and patient people who believed in me despite evidence to the contrary.

I covered mostly human-interest stories—stories about one-armed bowling champions and blind twins who golfed. I covered stories about Kurt Angle, a local boy and champion wrestler whose story was hard to muck up. When I had to do a real sports story, I'd come to my editors with statistics I didn't understand, and they'd explain the numbers without making me feel like the idiot I was. Then I'd go write, under deadline, pretending to know a thing about a thing I knew nothing about.

I still know little about sports, but I became a writer through the kindness and patience of others.

***

Like most Pittsburghers, I love the Steelers, despite my limited understanding of football. I grew up watching Franco. I loved that the Steelers won Super Bowls when Pittsburgh itself was floundering, our mills closing, so many people out of work and hope.

Franco, his toughness and talent, his kindness and patience, his humility and grace gave my city dignity. Franco's goodness became a metaphor for the best of Pittsburgh.

"I'm forever black and gold," Franco liked to say long after his Pittsburgh playing days were over.

For people like me, who don't understand the game, the Immaculate Reception was the one moment that cemented Franco's place in history, the one miracle I watched so many times on TV that I, like millions of other Pittsburgh Steelers fans, felt like I lived it. A playoff game in Pittsburgh vs. the nasty Oakland Raiders, time running out, the quarterback running around like a maniac trying to find somewhere to throw the ball, then throwing the ball, and the ball got batted, and Franco caught it an inch above the grass and sprinted for the endzone. Pittsburgh lost their minds with the joy and magic of watching greatness.

***

I got home safe. The popsicle was strawberry, I think, and it was delicious, so cold on my swollen flu-struck tongue. I went to bed and slept the rest of the day.

I didn't get fired. My bosses never said much about it. I think they even treated me a little more gently after that, the way people might treat someone who'd been blessed by the Pope.

When I saw Franco many years later and thanked him, he didn't remember helping me. Why would he? It was a tiny thing. A simple kindness to a clueless kid with the flu. It was, I think, just one in a string of too many kindnesses to count.

Everyone has a Franco story, it seems. Weeks after Franco's passing, I keep reading them—all those times he took a moment to sign an autograph or pose for a picture; all the times he was gentle and patient with fans and other players; the random Franco sightings on the airport shuttle at a Pittsburgh sandwich shop.

"It's almost impossible to process that he could give so much to so many people personally," Franco's son, Dok Harris, told ESPN. "People have been telling me stories about how they met him some time in 1977 or 1987 or 1991. It was important to them, and it made a difference in their lives. And that's really the beauty of my father, truly a very blessed soul who just really sought to help everybody out."

I keep thinking of a poem by another of my beloveds, Raymond Carver. The poem is called "Late Fragment." It goes like this:

And did you get what you wanted
from this life even so?
I did.
And what was it you wanted?
To call myself beloved.
To feel myself
beloved on this earth.

Dear Franco:
You are
beloved on this earth.

Wonder. Sunbeam. Bread. Loaf.

In the 1900s, I was in my 20s and on scholarship at a pinkie-up writers conference in Middlebury, Vermont. By the 1900s, I mean the 1990s, and by pinkie-up I mean a conference called Bread Loaf.

At first I thought the conference was called Bread Loaf to undercut the pinkie-upness of things. What's less pretentious than a loaf of bread? Wonder, Sunbeam, Schwebel's, Kings Hawaiian. But the conference, founded by Robert Frost, that pre-eminent poet of mending walls and pinkie-upness, is housed at Middlebury College and named for a mountain that presides over the campus like an artisanal rosemary sourdough bun.

The brilliant author John Irving was on the faculty of Bread Loaf that year. I love John Irving's books. Lots of people do. Think *The World According to Garp*, a book made into a movie about a nurse who wants a child but not a husband and who impregnates herself by raping a dying soldier who, though brain dead, has a perpetual erection and boom—a kid is born.

Think *The Cider House Rules*, a book made into a movie about the importance of women having bodily autonomy at a time when abortions were illegal and deadly and starring Charlize Theron's luminous bum.

Maybe you don't know John Irving or his books. I understand. The 1900s, the 90s in particular, sound like and are ancient times now.

"You kids today," my father, a child of the Great Depression, used to say. "You don't know what it's like. We used to strap cereal boxes to our shoes when the soles wore out. We thought ketchup was spaghetti sauce. There were bugs in the flour. There were bugs in the flour, and we liked it."

"You kids today," I hear myself say. "Put down the phone and read a book for god's sake."

One by John Irving, maybe.

"Okay, boomer," my Gen Z daughter Phelan says.

"Gen X," I say, and she says, "Whatever," and puts her headphones on.

***

Once generations are past, they're past, no matter what name we give them or how hard we try to hold onto the dignity of our former and current lives. Still, some things feel timeless. John Irving's books, for instance. And the movies. And the actors who play his characters.

Shine on into eternity, Charlize Theron and your golden bum.

***

John Irving, an alum and former wrestler from Phillips Exeter Academy, the sixth oldest private boarding school in the United States and a feeder school for Harvard and Yale, made a name for himself as a feminist ally through his books.

In the 1990s no one would have said "feminist ally." We would have said John Irving wrote good books about serious and heartfelt things, and we would have hoped, like many people do, that the artist, the person, was as good as his work.

It's a terrifying thing to meet your heroes, especially literary ones. Writers, I know because I've been around and because I am one, can be the worst. Maybe it's because the stakes are so low (hello, poets). Or maybe it's because writing is, like most art forms, an act of ego.

Exhibit A: the pronoun "I."

"I am large. I contain multitudes," Walt Whitman wrote, but he meant the opposite of ego. He meant we are all connected in the humbling and exalted experience of being human. The beauty of that.

Exhibit B: A famous poet I know, upset that he was not receiving an adequate stipend or sufficient adoration for his appearance at a place not unlike Bread Loaf, spitefully took a bite of every cookie his hosts laid out for his post-reading reception. Then he pulled the spigot on one of the containers filled with free punch and let the punch puddle-up.

Everyone seemed to think the poet was funny and charming, but I thought he was a jerk, even though I'd loved his poems and go on loving them still.

Those were good cookies. People would have enjoyed them, I think.

The punch was delicious.

Someone who was not the famous poet, who was not in charge of the famous poet's stipend or audience size, would have to mop up all that punch. The punch was sweet, so it left a sticky residue, a stain, something that would have to be cleaned by someone who was not the famous poet, someone on their hands and knees.

"Resist much, obey little," Walt Whitman said, and maybe the famous poet thought that gave him a pass. But Whitman said this, too, "Despise riches, give alms to everyone that asks, stand up for the stupid and crazy."

In other words, be kind. Don't eat other people's cookies. Don't make a mess if you're not willing to clean it up yourself. Be a good human.

***

But back to John Irving, the rockstar writer at a rockstar writers conference, where I, a working-class kid who had done my share of mopping, a 20-something human clueless about all the things John Irving lived and knew and seemed so certain about, was sure I didn't belong.

By scholarship, I mean I worked as a waitress serving food and drinks to rockstar writers like John Irving. My waitressing covered my Bread Loaf tuition, which would have been thousands of dollars I couldn't—and still couldn't—afford.

The current tuition for Bread Loaf is over $4,000 plus fees, which is about what I bring home every month now as a professor at a rickety branch campus of a major university that offers a $600 kick-back a year for "professional development," aka conferences like Bread Loaf.

I have two kids, a mortgage, gas bills, water bills, too many bills to count. If you're reading this, you probably have the same bills and maybe more. I live in the house I grew up in, in a rust-belt town just outside of Pittsburgh.

There is a certain amount of privilege that helps when you're trying to be a writer. It's not that you can't write without it, but—as Hemingway knew when he married a series of wealthy, wealthier, wealthiest, super-wealthiest-to-the-infinity-power wives—money and time are nice to have.

"Isn't it pretty to think so," Hemingway's Jake Barnes in *The Sun Also Rises* said about everything he imagined and longed for in the world—love, sex, a future to dream on.

The famous poet with the cookies? He came from my home country. He married an heiress to a wine fortune. He won many writing prizes.

***

Back in the 1990s, I and my fellow scholarship humans were dubbed Waitrons, like robots from *The Jetsons*.

"They don't call them that anymore," a young writer who's been to a more recent and more woke Bread Loaf told me. "It's classist and offensive."

The young writer who told me this was a recent graduate of The Iowa Writers Workshop. She was friends with a friend of the editor of *The Paris Review*, who she met while summering in the Hamptons. Anyone who uses summer as a verb is, to me, classist and offensive, but the young writer was sweet, and maybe a bit clueless about the 1990s, which my daughter calls the 1900s, which seems wrong, too ancient, then exactly right.

Of my fellow Waitrons, there were few working-class writers. One Waitron was the son of an award-winning poet. Another was the winner of a prestigious New York poetry prize. Most used summer as a verb. Most had studied with big-name writers at Ivy League universities that, where I was concerned, might as well have been on Mars.

***

Remember phone books? Remember the Yellow Pages? If you

were around in the 1990s and before, you do. Those were magic books, catalogs of human beings doing human things, humans living at addresses with landlines, a family sharing the same phone.

I don't mean to romanticize things, even when I do, but being a Waitron was anything but classist or offensive. It was an elite pathway into the next level of elite-ness, only I didn't know that then.

I'd waited tables since I was 12 years old at The Trafford Polish Club. I was good at it. I could manage 100-plus senior citizens who wanted fried fish sandwiches and boiled hot dogs and cheese balls. I could weave through rows of card tables like a dancer and rarely drop or spill a thing. I was proud of this. Arrogant, even.

Back then, you could find The Trafford Polish Club, and any other ethnic club in Pittsburgh, in The Yellow Pages. You could call and a wall phone would ring and maybe someone would pick it up, but probably not.

I worked bingo nights mostly, Mondays and Wednesdays, 5 p.m.-10 p.m. I made about $2 an hour, plus tips. I worked for my grandmother Ethel, a 300-plus-pound Slovak woman, who ran the kitchen like a gulag.

"We split 50/50," Ethel said. She'd pour out my tip jar at the end of each night and pretend to count.

I'm pretty sure my grandmother cheated me for years. I'm pretty sure she thought it was okay because I was adopted and not someone she needed to be honest with, genetically-speaking. I loved my grandmother and it would take years for me to realize she didn't love me back.

But that's another story.

The story I want to tell now is about Bread Loaf, and I believed I was a good writer who was good at waiting tables. I believed this was one thing that made me feel I belonged, my ability to write and to serve.

And John Irving wanted a glass of milk.

I'd navigated the Polish Club, that obstacle course of folding chairs, cigarette smoke-smog, the clouded sighs of septuagenarian bingo players bent fetal over cards that were most likely not winners. But something about bringing a glass of milk to John Irving, the great writer, tilted gravity.

What happened: I spilled milk in John Irving's lap. Then I tried to mop it with my apron. I dabbed and dabbed. It was, of course, awkward.

Sorry, John Irving.

Sorry I blotted your lap and may have touched you in a way that was unintentionally inappropriate. Not classist, but offensive. You're 80-plus now. I hope you've forgotten. Maybe you haven't forgotten though, because I haven't.

"Memory is a monster," John Irving wrote in *A Prayer for Owen Meany*, another classic. "You forget—it doesn't."

***

That I landed the Waitron scholarship was a miracle. People like me, from Trafford, Pennsylvania, didn't often end up at places like Bread Loaf, a luxurious retreat located in a billboard-free state famous for Ben & Jerry ice cream, maple syrup, and artisanal everything.

Artisanal, when most people use it now, is a synonym for expensive. Fancy. Pinkie up.

Growing up, I had my working-class practical plans: I learned to type; I spelled well enough to win spelling bees; I knew shorthand; I could wait tables; I could write; I studied journalism; I believed in the power of true stories and the Oxford comma and the who, what, when, where, why and how of things.

All those human skills and beliefs that now sometimes feel useless.

These days I make my living teaching writing. My students and their sweet parents want a sure thing, but nothing is sure now. Not the sciences. Not the humanities. Not humans. Nothing. But the sciences more than the humanities. Universities used to be cheap or free, there to educate and enlighten along with the practical skills that students needed for jobs. Now universities want to be expensive trade schools while talking about the humanities and cutting all the writing classes.

"You're our investment," my mother, a nurse, said when I was back in college, meaning she expected me to pay off, meaning, I think, that she expected me to do some good in this world. Or at least she expected me to make enough money so I wouldn't have to ask her for more.

Like Robert Frost, I play tennis, though Robert Frost was a notorious tennis cheat.

"Everyone knew to let Bob win," a regular at Bread Loaf told me. "He was a very sore loser."

"Writing free verse," Robert Frost said, "is like playing tennis with the net down."

"As the spirit wanes, the form appears," Charles Bukowski, that rough sweetheart, said.

But that's a writer's argument.

What I'm talking about here, mostly, is class.

My parents gave me tennis lessons. Expensive. My parents sent me to prep school. Expensive. I play piano. Expensive. I can almost speak a language other than English, and, because I worked for over seven years as a flight attendant—a Waitron in the sky—I have been to Turkey and Rome and the Greek Islands, where I felt connected to history through *The Odyssey* and *The Iliad*, books I read in graduate school with a professor who said I couldn't truly understand those books unless I read them in the original Greek.

I cannot read anything in the original Greek.

To help poor graduate students like me understand books like *The Canterbury Tales*, our professor, Dr. Hinman, brought in puppets. Alisoun, The Wife of Bath, was my favorite. Gap-toothed, deaf in one ear, she loved to insinuate herself into places she didn't belong.

"Except experience, mine, for what it's worth," the wife says. "And that's enough for me."

At Bread Loaf, I'd insinuated myself into places I didn't belong and had experiences to tell because of it. And I acted, like the Wife of Bath, terribly, more often than not.

***

Remember the famous poet who bit all the cookies? Remember how judge-y I was about that?

One night, a reporter from *USA Today* came to interview us Waitrons. She took us to an inn that was once the set for *The Bob Newhart Show*, starring comedian Bob Newhart as a gentle psychologist named Dr. Robert Hartley who was surrounded by a cast of characters that were, more or less, nuts.

The comedian Bob Newhart was famous for doing a phone bit where the audience could imagine a conversation between, say, Bob Newhart and King Kong, or Bob Newhart as Sam Hennessey, a maintenance worker who calls his boss at the Empire State Building because Sam Hennessey is worried about what to do with a giant ape whose toe is sticking through a window.

"I'm sure there's a rule against apes shaking the building," Sam Hennessey says, "Yes, sir. I said, 'Shoo ape.' I yelled at his feet. … but my jurisdiction only extends to his navel. … I thought maybe I could smear the Chrysler Building with bananas."

The Bob Newhart Inn was, and is, still famous, a Vermont landmark, sacred comic ground.

The reporter from *USA Today* bought us drinks and food on an expense account. She was young and sweet and naive, maybe on one of her first assignments. We were maybe, in hindsight, a little bitter. Or arrogant. Or, just like that famous poet I'd meet years later, jerks.

To dish out meals to famous writers whose lives we longed for felt less fulfilling as the days passed. We were invisible and nameless until a famous writer, one of our teachers in a conference, dubbed us worthy of being seen and named.

That night we ate. We drank. We stole expensive wine from the *The Bob Newhart Show* inn and stashed it in our backpacks and no one saw or said "shoo, apes" or bothered any of us much.

It was good wine. People who visited The Bob Newhart Inn might have enjoyed it. I don't know how that sweet reporter had to justify her expense account, how she had to clean up or be responsible for all of our messes. I'd like to apologize to her now, but that was many years ago and I don't remember her name.

Still, I'm sorry, lovely human.

I'm sorry I was arrogant and awful and I'd like to blame it on age and stupidity but really it was something else—entitlement, anger maybe, a misplaced sense of justice.

That night, under the Vermont stars, we drank Bob Newhart wine straight from the bottles and dreamed of our futures as famous writers whose work would change the world. When we said the world, we meant Earth, humankind.

***

One of my students, majoring in the sciences, recently tried to declare a major in creative writing. Her advisor, a science person, said, "Why? That's useless."

I'm trying hard to hold onto the things I believe keep me grounded in this life. Love. Poetry. Kindness. The way that writing, when we do it well and with full human hearts, allows us to connect with one another and makes the terrifying experience of living this mortal life less lonely.

How silly that sounds some days.

How it feels as essential as breathing.

"The future is no more uncertain than the present," dear Walt Whitman said.

***

Recently I sat in a public space with a purple typewriter and a sign that said, "Free poems. Any topic." It's a little vulnerable to sit in a public space offering poems on demand, but I wanted to prove something, my own value maybe. I wrote poems about a blind and deaf cockapoo, bees and sea monkeys and dust bunnies, best friends and sisters, toddlers with drum sets, and, of course, cats. As I clacked away, people sat across from me, no cell phones, just open, vulnerable humans sharing why they might want or need some words.

There were tears. There was hugging. There was laughter.

I don't think the poems I wrote were very good—they were flawed and messy, written on the fly like that—but no one seemed to mind. The poems I wrote were one-offs. There is no record of them beyond the moment, the poem equivalent, maybe, of the more beautiful sand mandalas Buddist monks make and then sweep away to show the impermanence of everything, but especially, maybe, human pride, hubris.

"I can't believe you don't make copies," my husband, a beautiful writer, said. He meant how important the act of creating is, how life-affirming, maybe. Something worth saving.

***

"Stop," John Irving said as I mopped his lap. "Just stop."

I did.

But I kept on writing, hoping one day it might matter some.

Family History Of X

When I was diagnosed with breast cancer, my doctor, Dr. Johnson, who looked like the late great comedian Norm MacDonald and told late-great-comedian jokes and liked to draw stick-figure breasts on a whiteboard to show surgical options, asked, "Do you have a family history?"

Dr. Johnson had already drawn a pair of disembodied breasts before he asked this. The breasts and nipples were squared off, like they'd been built with Legos.

"Like Doc Johnson?" I said, meaning Doc Johnson of sex toy fame.

I may have giggled. I was in my fifties, too old to giggle, but old enough to confront my mortality with jokes.

Two boobs and a cancer cell walk into a bar. A woman says, "I'll have a double."

Give it a minute.

Words writers should not use, according to Pulitzer Prize-winning novelist Elizabeth Strout: giggle, chuckle, guffaw. If you don't know Elizabeth Strout, read *Olive Kitteridge*. It's brilliant. If you don't know Doc Johnson, the Proctor & Gamble of porn, the company that models its sex toys based on the anatomy of adult-film stars like Jenna Jameson and Jeff Stryker, give it a Google.

When Jeff Stryker became a writer, he tried to sue a nightclub because the noise kept him from concentrating enough to finish his memoir. Jeff Stryker sued for the rights to a sex toy called Jeff Stryker's Cock and Balls, a dildo for which Stryker claimed intellectual property rights and called "an object of higher culture."

"Questions?" the real Dr. Johnson, the man who would save my life, said, and pointed his dry-erase marker at me, like he was calling on a student, like he hadn't heard that Doc Johnson thing hundreds of times, breast cancer being ubiquitous and all.

None of Dr. Johnson's drawings looked real. None of the drawings resembled my body, that traitor that was trying to kill me.

"My daughter loved Legos," I said as Doc Johnson drew another brick-breast and pretended, maybe, not to hear me.

Step on a Lego first thing in the morning, barefoot. Some days, that's how parenthood feels, and when I say parenthood, I mean life.

I'd been warned about Dr. Johnson's passion for sketching. When I called to make an appointment, Dr. Johnson's assistant said, "Doc likes to draw a lot."

I had no idea what she meant, so I said, "Okay?"

I said okay a lot back then. When another doctor showed me what she saw on my mammogram, tiny flecks that lined up like grains of rice in my left breast, when she called this concerning, a word neutral as oatmeal, I said, "Okay."

When a nurse called to confirm malignancy, I said, "Okay."

I may have thanked her.

I hope I did.

"Manners," the mother who raised and loved me, said. "Remember. Your problems are not other people's problems."

My mother was a nurse. She was tough and lovely and she died. Breast cancer. I am adopted. My mother's story is not my story.

About family history, I said, "I don't know," and Dr. Johnson held his marker mid-air and said, "Explain."

Dr. Johnson may have been a great artist. Home with his wife, who he called Mrs. Johnson, as in "Mrs. Johnson requires my presence at a gala and so I'm not scheduling surgeries then because I fear death," Dr. Johnson may have painted masterpieces. He may have painted happy little trees. He may have painted snowy mountains. But in his office, with his whiteboard, he was limited.

I was limited, too. I couldn't explain. Adopted people like me don't know their medical histories. It's something we must articulate on forms. Again and again.

History of cancer? Unknown.

History of heart disease? Unknown.

History of, history of—unknown, unknown.

I'd been adopted through Catholic Charities. When we met, my Catholic Charities social worker held my file—thick, redacted—though she couldn't let me see inside because that was the Catholic Charities rule. My file was so ordinary—a manila folder.

The social worker said, "Sometimes these things work out, like on Oprah. Most times they don't." Then she pushed my file across her desk, just out of reach.

The short version: I found my birth mother. I asked for a medical history. Maybe I wanted my birth mother to care a little. Maybe I wanted her to love me, even. Or love me enough to let me know if something in the genes she handed down would kill me.

My birth mother refused. Instead, she wished me dead. We talked through the internet, and she wished me dead.

"I'm adopted," I told Dr. Johnson, who said, "Ah!" and ordered genetic testing, which the insurance company would cover, considering.

Dr. Johnson sketched a single mastectomy. Double mastectomy. Lumpectomy with chemo and radiation and so on. He drew an image, then struck an X through it, and moved on to the next, and the next. X. X. X.

What I know about the first chapters of my life—X.

What I know about my birth mother—X.

What I know about what my daughter might face—no genetic predisposition for breast cancer. My cancer—likely environmental.

Still. X.

I decided upon a double mastectomy.

"Don't heal your pain. Amputate."

That's advice I'd gotten years before from a poet who wanted to teach me to write what was true and not settle for easy conclusions. She knew nothing about breasts, cancer, adoption, or children. She meant writing. I knew she meant writing. Later, it sounded stupid. I liked her still and nodded. I like her still and would still nod.

Later, when Dr. Johnson saw my husband in the waiting room before my surgery, my husband was reading a book of poems.

"You're going to need a bigger book," Dr. Johnson said and winked.

My surgery lasted 13 hours. It was the best sleep I had in years.

"When I go into surgery, I am completely Zen," a friend who has had many cancer surgeries told me later. "I feel peaceful. I feel fully myself."

One of my poet-teachers, Linda Pastan, wrote, "There is an age when you are most yourself."

Linda Pastan died, age 90, after complications from cancer surgery.

Jenna Jameson, XXX: Jenna Jameson, born to a police officer and a showgirl who died from cancer when Jenna was two; Jenna Jameson, whose mother's cancer treatments bankrupted her family and left Jenna and her brother to grow up in a trailer park, mostly alone; Jenna Jameson who was raped and abused and went on to become the unapologetic queen of porn, said, "Ultimately what matters is not the experiences you have at a young age, but whether or not you are equipped by your parents, your genetics, your education, to survive and deal with them."

I think about Jenna Jamison sometimes. I almost never watch porn. I like that it exists, that it makes people happy. I want people to be free and open. I am sometimes not that.

The double mastectomy I opted for included DIEP reconstruction. Dr. Johnson took away the cancer. My plastic surgeon, Dr. Gimbel, an elegant man whose staff looked like they popped from the set of *ER*, each one more beautiful than the next, re-built my breasts with fat he suctioned from my belly and hips.

Not everyone can have this surgery. You need just the right amount of fat in just the right spots. I was—chubby, curvy—a good specimen. Genetics. Whatever. Before my surgery, I had to stand against a wall and be photographed naked from the waist up.

"Don't worry, these won't show up on Facebook," Dr. Gimbel said, and winked.

Dr. Gimbel had some trouble with his camera. The photos took longer than expected. I stood there, exposed. Then turned right. Turned left.

"Posing nude," Jenna Jameson said, "is one of my favorite things to do in this world."

"It's all from the neck down," Dr. Gimbel said to make me comfortable.

My body, disembodied. No head, no face, nothing to connect it to me at all.

What a Doll

One Christmas, when I was very young, I asked my parents for a sister. Because I'd been adopted, I figured getting a sister was easy, like going to the grocery store, like picking out melons.

My parents got me a life-size doll named Suzie. Suzie was a My Twin doll—blonde, like me, green-eyed, like me—and when I held her hand Suzie would walk with me, stiff as Frankenstein.

My dark-haired, dark-eyed parents had special-ordered Suzie and Suzie was expensive, they said. Everything about me was expensive, I knew, because my parents often told me. I was often in casts to my waist and had many surgeries so that I'd be able to walk right and not like Suzie.

The doctor's bills were why I couldn't have the sister I wanted. The doctor's bills and the food bills and the clothes bills and the mortgage and the bills to fix the car my father wrecked that time he stopped at the bar after work.

Besides, my parents said, sisters were overrated, and I already had a dog. Both my parents had sisters they didn't like much. My mother's sisters would make her hide in the attic as a teenager when their boyfriends came to visit because she was too pretty. My father's sisters fought about money and the good china left behind when their parents died.

"Sibling rivalry," my mother said, and blotted her pink lipstick.

"Bloodsuckers," my father, the millworker said, though he loved his sisters despite all that.

"Why can't you be satisfied?" my dissatisfied mother would say and sigh.

"Just be grateful already," my tired father would say. "Without us, you'd have nothing."

I was, according to my parents and my aunts and the teller at Mellon Bank and the nuns at St. Regis Catholic School, the opposite of grateful. I was stubborn and hardheaded. I read too many books. I broke things like crayons and my mother's ceramic poodles. Once, in kindergarten, I'd stolen another kid's slide rule and refused to hand it over. I talked back some.

"Be careful," my mother said, "or we'll send you back where you came from."

Where that was, I didn't know then, but I'd seen orphanages on TV, the babies in cribs lined up like an assembly line, the dirty-faced Dickens' orphans in their ratty bunk beds begging for gruel, the headmistresses all in black, rulers where their hands should be.

Christmas didn't come for orphans, I knew, Orphan Annie aside, and so when my parents presented me with Suzie, I thanked them over and over and over until they asked me to stop.

"You always have to over-do things," my mother said and sighed more.

Suzie, though, was a model child. She sat when she was supposed to sit and she didn't squirm when her hair was brushed and she didn't want expensive cereal just for the toy inside. More than that, Suzie didn't talk, which, according to my mother, was the best thing of all.

My mother called Suzie and me *the girls*. She dressed Suzie up in my pink pajamas. She'd give Suzie my underwear, which was creepy since Suzie was smooth as a light bulb down there. My mother did our hair so we matched, high ponytails, pigtailed braids.

I'd prop Suzie at the kitchen table or in front of our big console TV and sometimes my mother would think it was me there and not Suzie. Other times she'd mistake me for Suzie and when I moved my mother would startle.

"You'll give me a heart attack one of these days," she'd say, but I thought Suzie was the one.

This was years before *Chucky* and *Poltergeist* and *Bride of Chucky* and so on. Suzie was terrifying before terrifying dolls were mainstream.

Still, I wanted to be the daughter my parents had wanted and paid for. I wanted to be good and grateful, to not fuss so much. And so I tucked Suzie into bed beside me every night and my mother would make me say a prayer—"If I die before I wake..." —and she'd kiss my forehead and Suzie's forehead and click on a Donald Duck nightlight.

I lay awake in the dark and imagined another life for myself, a place with a real sister, a place where I fit and wouldn't have to pretend so much. A place for everything and everyone in their place, my mother who mixed her metaphors liked to say.

Suzie lay awake, too. Her eyes were supposed to click closed when she lay down, but they only ever went halfway, like she was suspicious, like she was biding time, like she was waiting for me to close my eyes first.

Hopeful Things

*"I hate the sight of men in their cups who shout…'Have some more!
Drink up!'"*—Sei Shonagon (c966-1017),"Hateful Things."

The guy at Krick's Tavern holds up a middle finger in front of the big screen TV so his finger casts a shadow over everyone, especially the Pittsburgh Pirates who, for once, are winning.

The miracle of that.

From outside, Krick's looks like the kind of place that would play Fox News on a loop and new-country songs about kick-ass trucks on the jukebox. But inside Krick's, Fox News seems as distant as Mars. Here there's only sports on the TV and 80s hair metal on the jukebox.

This is Trafford, Pennsylvania, a tiny slice of Northern Appalachia, no elegy necessary.

Trafford, Pennsylvania—the last stop in Pittsburgh's Electric Valley, a town founded by George Westinghouse, who said "If someday they say of me that in my work I have contributed something to the welfare and happiness of my fellow man, I shall be satisfied."

And tonight, Krick's, a dive bar in a dive town, my divetown hometown, my rust-belt country, is packed.

Even though I live here, it's my first time at Krick's. I can be judge-y. Outside, Krick's, like most bars in town, looks rough—rusted fire escape, rickety screen door, glass block windows, a sign that says, "Smokers Welcome."

It's not a place I'd usually go. I've grown fancy and soft, all wine-bar-ish and artisanal, despite my Trafford working-class roots. I moved away for years. I lived in New York City, and some days I still carry the arrogance of that like a designer purse or the way New Yorkers say "the city" and mean there's only one worth mentioning.

"Homing pigeons," a man in a fancy New York bar called Pittsburghers like me. "You move away, you move back. You can't help it."

My father was dying. I came back and, when it may have been possible for me to leave again, I stayed for reasons too many to count. Now a decorative license plate shaped like the state of Pennsylvania graces the bumper of my used Chevy Trax. It reads: Home. There's a star where Pittsburgh would be. The plate is one way to recognize my car in the landscape of nearly identical cars in the Wal-Mart parking lot.

My husband bought the license plate. He has a tattoo to match, though instead of a star to mark Pittsburgh, there's a blue-and-green globe, the world he loves carved into his skin.

Today, regarding Krick's Tavern, it's my husband who wants to be here.

"It's close to home and cheap," he said. "No drinking and driving."

My husband got a DUI when he was in his twenties, coming home from a party. He worked as a trucker back then and the DUI made a mess of his life. Now my husband, 30 years later, is more responsible. He also loves dive bars.

On one of our first dates, he took me to another dive bar, this one in his own hometown a few miles from Trafford, off Route 30. The Irwin Hotel, from the outside, looked run-down and scary, but inside the regulars were beautiful. A man who looked like Sam Elliott wore a leather hat and boots. The Irwin Hotel's Sam Elliott was in love with a woman who was trying to make him jealous by flirting with another regular, not nearly as handsome. Sam Elliott leaned back in his bar stool and said many things that night about love and violence and heartbreak I wish I remembered now.

What I know: The Irwin Hotel bartender was sweet. Sam Elliott, drunk, stoned, said gentle true things and though I already loved my husband, I loved him more for taking me there.

"Date night?" I said about going to Krick's. "Okay, whatever. My hangover's on you."

When I get angry about the lies people like J.D. Vance spread about Appalachia, or about the assumptions strangers make about the place I'm from and about the people who live here, I should start with myself. I'm a writer and, dear god, a college professor. I'm conflicted about my home in the way the great playwright August Wilson was conflicted about Pittsburgh.

"This is my home and at times I find it tremendously exciting," August Wilson said in an interview in 1994. "Other times I want to catch the first thing out that has wheels."

My husband, that lover of dive bars, is a writer and a college professor too. I've taught for 25 years. He's been a professor for two. Our journeys to being professors were wildly different but we've both worked many other jobs. Me: waitress, caterer, flight attendant, journalist, PR hack. Him: truck driver, slaughterhouse worker, social worker, burger-flipper. There are others, too many to mention.

In one of his novels, my husband wrote: "In Pittsburgh, you are tough or you are not…You start hearts or allow hearts to wind down like old clocks. I almost never think about what Pittsburgh means because I know it."

See why I love him?

Krick's is not anything I imagined it would be. The bar is polished wood and brass. The spotless bathrooms smell like fresh-cut flowers. Happy Hour starts at 7 p.m. and runs to 11. Here, no matter what politicians or pundits or the media say, no one talks politics, not even three months out from an election that has torn the rest of this country apart, not even the guy with the middle finger raised like a flag, who is pissed and pissed off and who's probably been drinking since noon.

The bartender—long glossy black hair, dark eyeliner, silver press-on nails—says, "Now Jerry, be nice," and keeps everyone else's drinks coming. She moves like a dancer in a boozy ballet. She moves like a crow with angel wings. Happy Hour means $2.50 domestics. It means $7 Sgambetti's pizza, pretty much a dough shell slathered in tomato sauce but, everyone at the bar agrees, still tasty.

You almost have to be from here to pronounce Sgambetti's.

You almost have to be from here to know what hope looks like:

Krick's new deck seating with fancy umbrella tables; Krick's new cocktail menu; the way an older woman at the other end of Krick's bar, her white hair done in dollops of whipped-cream curls, raises one of those new cocktails, a Mojito I think, fresh mint even, and pinkie-up wishes Jerry at the other end a safe trip home.

She calls him sweetheart.

"You be careful, sweetheart," she says, "Tomorrow is another day."

What hope is: tomorrow, another day.

You almost have to be from here to see Jerry and not a Yinzer, a hillbilly, a jagoff. You almost have to be from here to see the complexity of the man who smoothes his raggedy beard twice, then pats his pockets for his keys and wallet and cigarettes, before he turns to all of us at the bar and raises his finger again and says, "Screw you and you and you," that middle finger like a gun but almost sweet-like, maybe, like this is Jerry's way of saying "Have a good night!" and also "Tell your mama I said hi!"

Who knows what's in anyone's heart? Jesus or internet psychics, maybe, but politicians? Never.

Days from now a kid not old enough to drink here, from a town not far from here, will take a real gun, an AK, a gun politicians rallied for, to a political rally. People will die. None of them will be politicians, none of them will be regulars on Fox News or CNN or NPR. The dead will include a father who'd also been a firefighter. The dead will include the kid who wished death for others and who instead will lie dead on a rooftop. Two other people will be seriously injured. Others—too many to count— will carry the trauma of that day like stones in their throats.

On the news, bystanders will lift beers and cartons of Turner's Tea and stand around looking at the kid's dead body like they're watching a baseball game or waiting for some terrible movie to play out. There will be videos: the kid getting his high school diploma and smiling to "some applause," *The New York Times* will report.

Imagine the kids' parents. Imagine the family of the dead father who shielded his daughter and wife from bullets meant for someone else.

"Fight, fight," the politician will say, and pump his fist and invoke God.

"Chickens coming home to roost," Malcolm X said about violence before he was killed.

"Violence breeds violence, repression brings retaliation, and only a cleaning of our whole society can remove this sickness from our soul," Robert Kennedy said before he was killed.

But for now, let's push aside the news and soundbites and ominous quotes.

Let's focus on Jerry, his stupid middle finger rising up like Stonehenge. The way his finger stands like a prophet, proselytizing—what a word.

Jerry's finger, standing in judgment of us all.

And then the screen door of Krick's Tavern slams shut and Jerry's gone. No one says a word. No one says, "Screw you Jerry," or even "Good riddance." The beautiful bartender goes on dancing. No one at the bar has to wait for a drink and everyone seems happy.

The miracle of that.

The Irwin Hotel? It burned down years ago. A man who lived in the rooming house tried to make breakfast—fried eggs on a hot plate. The hot plate caught fire. Where the Irwin Hotel used to stand there's a fancy dining car. It's supposed to look historic, but it's new I think, shining silver and red. The dining car hosts receptions after shows at the theater next door. The theater is called The Lamp. On the roof of the building, there's a huge sculpture, Aladdin's Lamp, gold and glistening.

If you had three wishes for this world, what would you wish? Take a minute.

"I've got to stop pretending I'm something I'm not," the Genie in Aladdin said.

"Oh to be free!" the Genie said that, too, his one wish.

In between jukebox songs at Krick's, I eavesdrop on a couple in matching yellow work shirts.

"I watched my mother die, then I watched my father die," the man says, punctuating his words with a cigarette. "Ain't nothing can phase me after that."

I watched my mother die. I watched my father die. My father's last words: "Don't worry, sweetheart. I'll be around."

Sometimes I see my father everywhere—an old man shuffling in a crosswalk, a young man with his hands clenched on a steer-ing wheel, the man with the cigarette who repeats himself the way my father repeated himself because he believed no one ever heard him.

"Ain't nothing can phase me," the man says, "nothing after that," and stubs out his cigarette on the edge of the bar, then wipes the ash away with his thumb.

On Florida vacations, my father would stock up on cigarettes, Pall Malls, Lucky Strikes, Kools, my mother's brand. He'd buy carton after carton and load up the trunk of his Chrysler. He'd freeze the cartons and have enough cigarettes to last him a year.

These days, people in my hometown go to jail for taking cigarettes across state lines or selling them from the trunks of their cars. These days, most things people like my father and the people in Krick's Tavern might do to get by or get ahead would get them in trouble.

"I'll show all those cockroaches," my father would say about his bosses at the mill. "I'm a survivor."

"I'm lucky," my father would say. Then he'd call his bookie or go to Atlantic City and take the loss.

My father died. Lung cancer—the mills, the cigarettes, the losses, the sadness, the drinking, the giving up drinking, who knows.

"What caused it?" people ask when something terrible happens, as if living and dying were equations to be solved.

I've always been hopeless at math.

At Krick's Tavern, there's an old cigarette machine, the kind where you have to pull a lever to get the pack you want. The bartender keeps serving and the regulars keep drinking. The Pirates are winning for now. The Trivia Quiz over the bar asks, "How many colors are in a rainbow?" The answer: Seven.

Seven, the number of wisdom and intuition. Seven, the bridge between the mortal realm and higher places. Seven, the angel number, slot-machine lucky, God's magic digit.

The cigarettes in the old-school machine cost $14 a pack. Seven times two. Even I can do that math.

Who's lucky enough to afford that? Elon Musk maybe. Mars dollars.

$14 a pack is more than the minimum wage.

$14 a pack may save lives because many people who like to smoke can't afford to buy the things that will help kill them, and the people who can afford to smoke mostly vape instead.

"As more affluent people gave up the habit, the war on smoking, which was always presented as an entirely benevolent effort, began to look like a war on the working class," Barbara Ehrenreich, author of "Nickle and Dimed: On (Not) Getting By in America," explained. "You can't smoke indoors anymore. There goes the working-class bar. Where are these working-class bars now?"

Barbara Ehrenreich's been dead over a year now. If she were alive, I'd like to tell her "Trafford, Pennsylvania" and buy her a beer at Krick's, where right this minute the lovely bartender is bringing the lady with the whipped-cream hair another cocktail. The lady blows a kiss, first to the bartender, and then to the ceiling like she's making a wish that will fall down like confetti and bless all of us here.

The man in the yellow shirt lights another cigarette and offers one to the woman next to him.

The final score of the Pirates game comes across the screen— Pirates 4, White Sox 1, and everyone agrees this is good news, whether they care about baseball or not.

"Last call," the bartender at Krick's says. "Drink up!" But I think she's joking. It's still early. There's still time.

Spring Cleaning

The mildewed boxes in our basement nagged my husband New-man for decades. Newman is the organized type. He organizes our house in a way that I find amazing, then I accidentally wreck it, then he fixes it again. Sometimes he says, "Stop it." Other times, he says, "Stop messing shit up." I want to stop messing shit up. I'm messy.

My husband is gentle and sweet, despite appearances. His goatee comes to a point at his collarbone, regulation Hell's Angel chic. He swears so much no one, not even our kids, notices he swears. He has several tattoos and loves to tell fight stories. Still, he's a sweetheart—except when it comes to clutter. Then he's ruthless, a biker-bearded bully—which is good since, left to my own de-vices, our house would be overrun.

"I like order," Newman says, because so much else in life is be-yond our control.

I get it. He's a writer. I'm a writer. Too much clutter is distract-ing, the world being too much with us, so it goes. I leave stuff everywhere, cups, plates, towels. He says, "I don't want to clean, I want to write." I make more messes. I put a bag of cheese in a cabinet. I put a pot holder in the cheese drawer. "I'm distracted," I say, because I also want to write, because writing for me means thinking about writing when I should be thinking about other things, like putting cheese where it belongs.

"Not that it was beautiful / but that, in the end, there was / a certain sense of order there," the poet Anne Sexton wrote.

I love Anne Sexton. But, one day, Anne Sexton came home to her own tidy space. She put on her dead mother's fur coat, took off her own rings (poets love rings), poured a glass of vodka—

that tidiest of drinks—locked herself in her garage, started her car and gassed herself to death.

As role models go, Anne Sexton is a major fail.

But this isn't about that.

"Do we really need all of these?" Newman says, holding up the stack of hats our son, Locklin, wore from age 1 to 10, little denim bucket hats I keep layered like Russian nesting dolls in our hall closet.

Sometimes I line the hats up, from tiniest to least tiny, like a timeline of my son's joy. When he stopped loving hats, the sadness crept in—adolescence, the embarrassment of loving anything too much.

"The Before Times," people say about the line between light and dark, between innocence and experience.

Other things I've stashed: my children's teeth—creepy and which occasionally draw some sort of bugs I don't want to understand; my dead parents' expired passports; a blue handkerchief my father kept tucked in the pocket of his work pants; a souvenir penny of Detroit my grandmother left me in her will.

I don't think of myself as a hoarder.

This may be the first of the five stages of hoarding. Denial. Acceptance. Whatever else. I love stuff. I collect it. I hold it. I hope you have stuff, but not too much. Just enough to hold the memories that matter close.

As for the boxes, I kept them stacked next to our washer and dryer, hoping they wouldn't draw Newman's attention. After years, the stack reached almost to the basement ceiling, but it was my stack, my boxes. I wanted to keep them.

"My life is in those boxes," I said, like an actress in a 1940s movie about to faint or break into song.

"Oh please," Newman said.

"Those are my memories," I replied—and realized that was the same excuse I used when I was 12 and my mother demanded I clean my room.

"Your memories take up too much space," my mother said. "Either they go or you do."

I was an adopted kid, so this threat hit different.

My mother didn't mean it, of course, but she liked order, too. Her generation washed walls and spring cleaned, that act of renewal, rebirth. My mother purged. She moved furniture around.

My mother believed moving a couch was a fresh start.

"Now isn't that better?" she said, her face lit with hope.

My mother believed moving a couch or a bed brought happiness, a new perspective, more possibilities for joy.

Maybe it did.

"I never seemed to like spring for what it was; I always loved it for what it might have been," Anne Sexton wrote.

Finally, after 22 years together, just before spring hit, tired, I gave in to Newman's sense of order.

"Do whatever," I said about the boxes.

Newman built a fire in our firepit. I helped him lug the boxes out. We fed the fire. There was so much paper—yellowed news clippings from my first work as a journalist, obscure literary magazines where I published embarrassingly terrible poems, fly-ers with my face on them, letters and printed-out emails from friends and kind strangers and former students who wrote to tell me something I'd done in this life mattered once.

At first, I hung back and let Newman handle things. Then I got in there. I read everything before I dropped it into the flames. I pulled a clipping of a story I wrote about a blind champion bowl-er; I pulled a clipping of a column I wrote about Live Aid and my first love and how we traveled to Philadelphia in the back of a Le Car driven by a scalper. I pulled poster after poster promoting my first book, my second, my third and so on. I burned dossiers, which is a fancy word for boxes of paper hoarded by academics who want to prove their worth in this world and get tenure for it.

What a word—tenure.

Tenure: the act, right, manner, or term of holding something.

As I watched everything burn, I wondered what I was holding onto, why it mattered, and why it felt, in the end, so freeing to let it go.

"Put your ear down close to your soul and listen hard," Anne Sexton wrote.

Listen.

Life is fleeting. Nothing will give us tenure in this world.

"I'm shredding my journals," the author Elizabeth Strout told me recently. Elizabeth Strout is a beautiful human, a Pulitzer Prize-winning writer, the subject of countless academic studies.

"I couldn't bear for anyone to see them," she said about her journals. "It's so personal."

Elizabeth Strout. People would want to read her biography, written by someone who studied her journals and notes and boxes of memories. But Elizabeth Strout is a private person. There is something beautifully invisible about her. She enters and leaves a room without people noticing. Her eyes, the color of the sea, are so intense, a camera focused on the world beyond her. She takes everyone else in.

"We all have to have something that's our own," Elizabeth Strout said. "And we have the right to make it disappear."

I have the right to make it disappear, I thought, as I poked the glowing embers of my life with a stick. I have the right to make it disappear, I thought, as I fed more paper to the flames.

P.S.

About those skates.

Like most writers, I side-gig a lot. In one side-gig, I teach doctoral students in the creative writing program at a theological seminary. Many of my students already have multiple degrees from Ivy League schools. Others travel the world and go into war zones to help people. Most are pastors. One is a chef. Another has walked the Camino de Santiago, a 500-plus mile pilgrimage in Spain that leads to the tomb of the apostle James the Greater in Santiago de Compostela, twice.

Twice.

I have never had the kind of faith that would lead me to walk 1000 miles to anywhere. I'm lucky if I get the 10,000 steps a day my Fitbit says I need to go on breathing. The good I can offer others is limited by my lack of skills and my selfish love of comfort. As I write this, I am sitting in a Lazy Boy recliner in a warm room, surrounded by books and wearing a plushy robe I just bought at Target. The robe wasn't even on sale.

I am, in short, a horribly flawed human who gets to work with brilliant, kind humans who inspire me to maybe one day be a less-flawed human. I'm grateful.

I know.

The skates.

I'm getting there.

At the end of their doctoral program, my students give public readings from their manuscripts. Their families and friends all come out for this.

One of my students, K., told me she grew up skating with her mom. Her mom was a high school teacher. After school, to shake off the day or just for joy, her mom would strap on skates and whip through the halls, the smooth slick floors and maze of locker-lined corridors a skater's dream.

Some days, K. would join her mother and the two of them would zip around, with K. sworn to secrecy because the principal would not like the idea of his high school turned into a roller rink.

For weeks before the reading, I'd lie awake and think about what I could give my students as graduation gifts.Everything I thought of seemed shallow and insufficient. What do you get a person who willingly walks 500 miles in search of peace and enlightenment?

Then I thought about K.

I should give K. the skates. Perfect. Then I'd think, "I don't want to give K. the skates." And the two parts of myself would go around like that, bickering like cartoon angels and devils.

It wasn't just that I didn't want to part with what were the sweetest pair of skates I'd ever seen. (Did I mention they were holographic?) Giving up the skates meant more. Surrender, I guess.

"There is an age when you are most yourself," my beloved teacher Linda Pastan said.

I knew I'd reached that age, but I kept fighting all the way up until the day of the reading. Then I put the skates in a gift bag. I handed them over to K., who showed them to her mother, who seemed about my age but perfect, like she just stepped out of a J.Crew catalogue. K.'s mother clapped her hands in delight.

"You're going to have to share," she said, and I wanted to grab the skates back, precious my precious, but didn't.

What K. did next: she put on the skates. K. is placid and serious as a stop sign. She's also the funniest person I've ever met.

She put on the skates and when it was her turn to read, she wheeled up to the podium. She was wearing a perfectly tailored suit. Her hair was glossed, not a strand out of place. She may even have been wearing pearls.

K. began reading, not missing a beat and never mentioning or even acknowledging that she had just skated up to a very serious podium in a very serious chapel on the campus of a seminary in which she was about to receive her latest degree.

When she finished, K. rolled back to her seat. A true professional, she didn't have to catch her balance even once.

"I am learning to abandon the world, before it can abandon me," Linda Pastan wrote that, too. But abandon is such a sad word, and what I feel isn't exactly that.

Remember I said I love comfort? Maybe that's the word I need. Comfort and joy. Lines from a Christmas hymn I knew by heart when I was a child and believed many things I've forgotten until now.

K. went on to become a dean at Princeton. I like to imagine her after a long day. She puts on the skates. She wheels through the prestigious halls, all that wood and marble, past the portraits of the theologians and philosophers and academics that have come before her, with the Village People's "Y.M.C.A." playing on repeat through her ear buds.

Publication Notes

Thanks to the editors of the following publications in which several of these essays first appeared, some in different forms: *Pittsburgh Magazine, Belt Magazine, The Washington Post, The Pittsburgh Post-Gazette, Drunk Monkeys, Pittsburgh Quarterly, The Journal of the Plague Years, Janice Magazine.* Thanks to Roadside Press and the wonderful Michele McDannold. Thanks to Sylvia Catello for your friendship, love, and enduring humor. Let's go crazy together forever. Thanks to Newman, you gravity-defying miracle heart. Here's to all the good years with years to go. And thanks to Locklin and Phelan. I love you more. More.

Lori Jakiela is the author of seven books, most recently a memoir, *They Write Your Name on a Grain of Rice: On Cancer, Love, and Living Even So* (Atticus Books). Another memoir, *Belief Is Its Own Kind of Truth, Maybe* (Autumn House Press), received the Saroyan Prize for International Literature from Stanford University. Lori's essay collection, *Portrait of the Artist as a Bingo Worker: On Work and the Writing Life* (Bottom Dog Press), has been adopted as a common text at Westmoreland Community College for the past two years. Many of the essays in *All Skate: True Stories from Mid-Life* have been published in places like *Pittsburgh Magazine, The Pittsburgh Post-Gazette, The Washington Post, Vol. 1 Brooklyn, Journal of the Plague Years, Pulse,* and more. Her other work has appeared in *The New York Times/Modern Love* column, *The Chicago Tribune, Brevity/Creative Nonfiction, Full Grown People, The Rumpus,* and more. Her author website is http://lorijakiela.net.

9 798899 054665